VOLUME 02

"Before the internet, if you didn't have the record, you couldn't play it. Back then, tracking down certain records could take a decade, and some remained elusive. This is why DJs had no problem playing their stuff on the radio – no one could copy them. Music recognition apps didn't exist. A side effect of the internet has been the breaking of the dictates set by the record. Every time I take an old record off the shelf, it's like a musical revival."

DJ Mad

Beginner, Radio DJ and vinyl collector

Hip hop is a mix of art and authenticity – and as much a visual expression as it is a musical revolution. The unique styles of hip hop culture resonate deeply with an ever-growing international fanbase and impact fashion, design, dance, art, and attitudes. The stylistic evolution represented in this second volume of The Art of Hip Hop Covers also illustrates the development of the music. Enjoy tons of street art, (out)dated fashions and poses, all kinds of weapons, cars, girls, not to forget the occasional 'visual sample': DJ Hurricane's The Hurra takes more than a little inspiration from the Blue Note cover of Art Blakey & The Jazz Messengers' Indestructible from the 1960s, while DJ Adlib's Adlibertine is almost indistinguishable from jazz vibist Mike Mainieri's Journey Through An Electric Tube from 1968. The machismo and misogyny of the oldest album cover in this collection, comedic rhymester Rudy Ray Moore's The Cockpit, give way to a gigantic Tyler, the Creator in shorts and a proper angel blue cardigan on Call Me If You Get Lost 51 years later.

A real black panther with a heavy rope gold chain on the cover of a late '80s LL Cool J album roars two calendar weeks (and 30 years) apart from the iconic Pink Panther with a green bead necklace and a Dipset pendant on the Gangster Music Vol.1 compilation. Speaking of Panthers: Among the many artworks featured on these covers, by artists as famous as Keith Haring, the one for The Last Poets' Chastisement from 1972 clearly stands out. Created by Jim 'Seitu' Dyson, 'one of the most significant graphic artists of the Black Power movement' (Afropunk), it shows seven black avenging angels descending from the darkened heavens to slaughter the golden calf and its light-skinned, fox-faced, devil- and money-worshipping guardians. The message of this artwork and album connects straight to Public Enemy's Muse Sick-n-Hour Mess Age from 1994, the politically charged suicidal skeleton on the cover of which was drawn by comic artist Mark Texeira – among whose comic book credits is also that for Vol. 3 of Marvel's Black Panther series. There's a lot to discover in this great year looking back on hip hop's past, take it day by day, cover by cover, album by album.

Götz Bühler

Journalist (ByteFM, Jazz thing), artistic advisor to the jazzahead! trade fair, conference and festival

SCAN THE SPOTIFY CODES TO PLAY EVERY ALBUM INSTANTLY! *

1.

Click the search bar in your **Spotify** app.
Then tip the camera icon at the top right.

2.

Scan the printed **Spotify**
code on the calendar page.

3.

Enjoy the music!

** Please note: Not all bands present themselves on Spotify, so there are various albums without a code.*

* Jan 1st, 1974
Michael Hampton
Orlando (Florida)

D.J. Magic Mike
It's Automatic
Cheetah Records, 1991
Cover Artists Unknown

01 JAN

Jungle Brothers
Because I Got It Like That
Gee Street, 1990
Bite it! (Design)
Donald Christie (Photo)

02 JAN

A Tribe Called Quest
Scenario
Jive, 1992
ZombArt NG (Design)
Jim Swaffield (Photo)

03 JAN

Fischmob
Männer können seine Gefühle nicht zeigen
Plattenmeister, 1995
Andrea Joerdens, Daniel Sommer, Marc Clausen (Design)
Dieter Gruber (Photo)

04 JAN

MC Shy D
I Wanna Dance
Luke Skyywalker Records, 1987
Cover Artists Unknown

05 JAN

Run DMC
Tougher Than Leather
Profile Records, 1988
Janet Perr (Design)
Robert Lewis (Photo)

06 JAN

Black Moon
Jump Up
Duck Down, 1999
Cover Artists Unknown

07 JAN

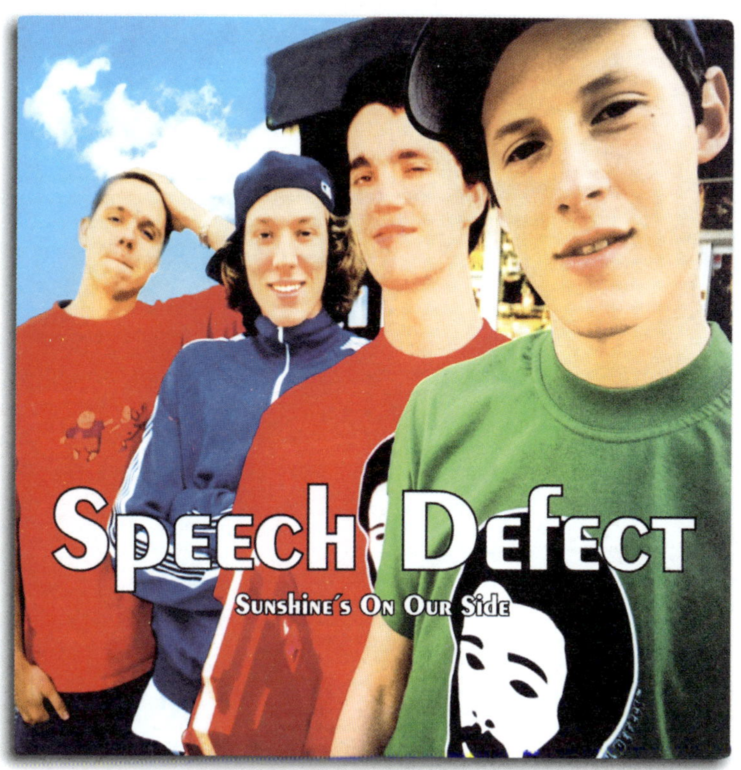

Speech Defect
Sunshine's On Our Side
No Cool Music, 2001
Thage (Design)
Martin Svensson (Photo)

08 JAN

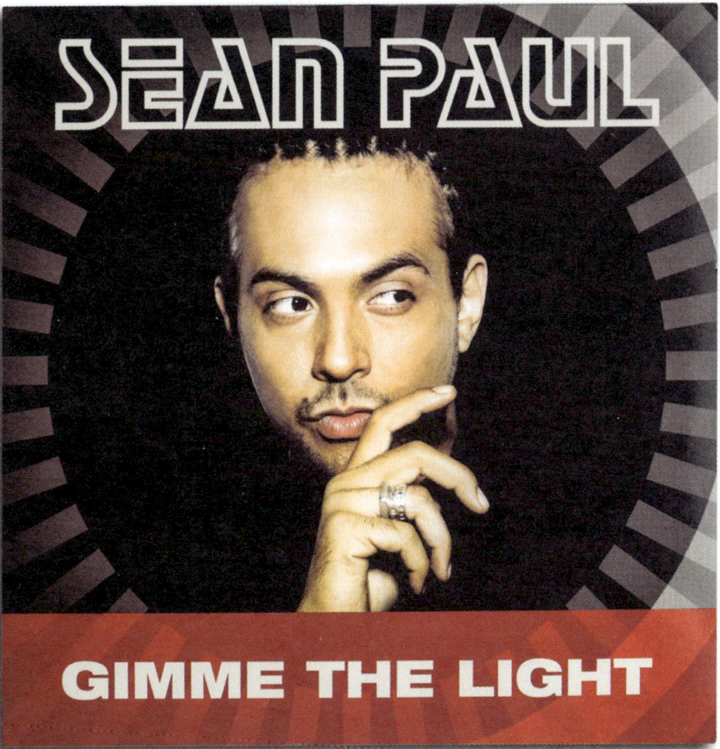

* Jan 9th, 1973
Sean Paul Ryan Francis Henriques
Kingston (Jamaica)

Sean Paul
Gimme The Light
VP Records, 2003
Cover Artists Unknown

09 JAN

The Beatnuts
The Spot (The Beatnuts Remix EP)
Relativity, 1998
Steven Chin Liu, Invisible Man (Design)
Invisible Man, Joseph Albaladejo (Photo)

10 JAN

* Jan 11th, 1971
Mary Jane Blige
New York City (USA)

Mary J Blige
Real Love
Uptown Records, 1992
Cover Artists Unknown

11 JAN

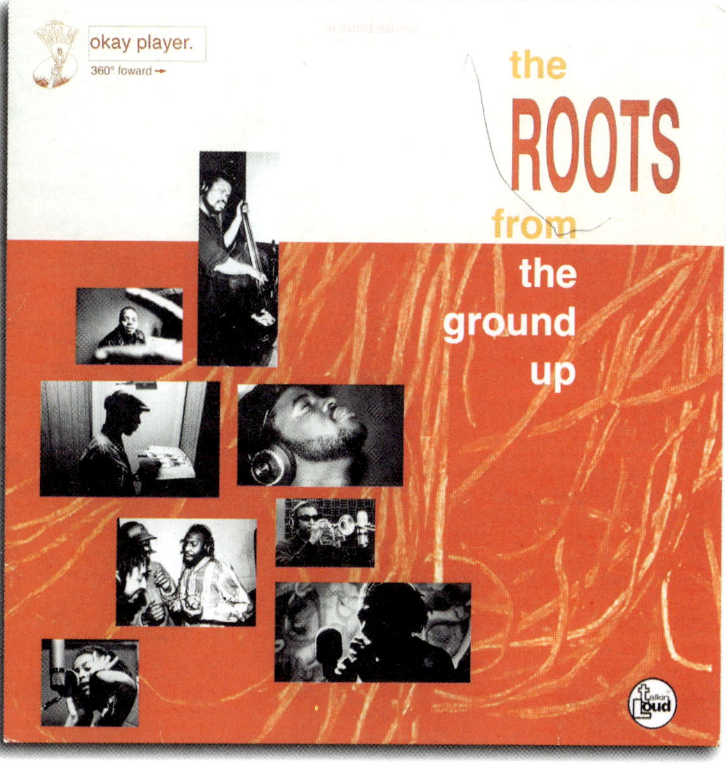

The Roots
From The Ground Up
Talkin' Loud, 1994
Cover Artists Unknown

Les Little
Les Vrais
Mercury, 1992
Cover Artists Unknown

13 JAN

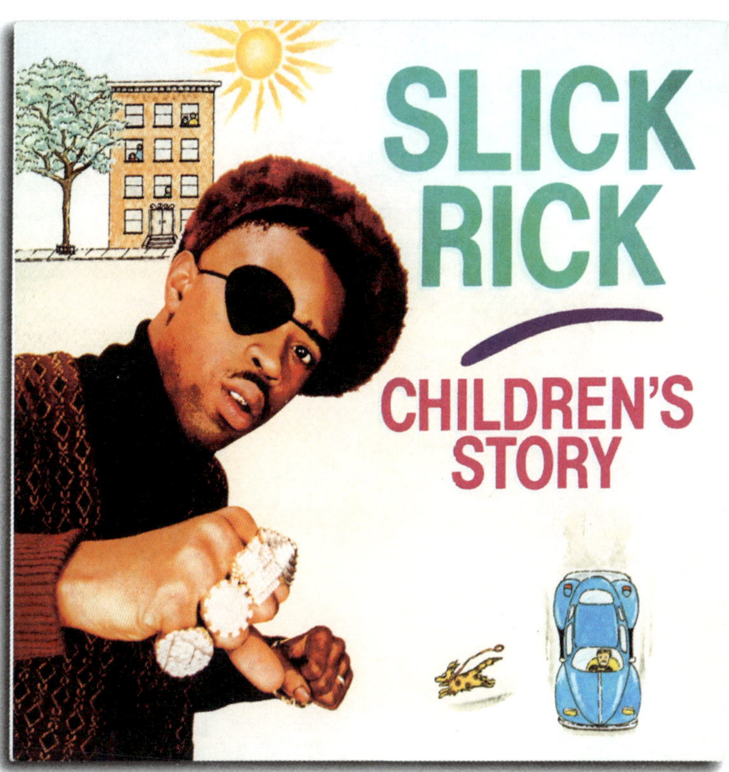

* Jan 14th, 1965
Richard Walters
London (UK)

Slick Rick
Children's Story
Def Jam Recordings, 1988
John Niccolls (Design)
Alcindor's Studio (Photo)

14 JAN

L.L. Cool J
Walking With A Panther
Def Jam Recordings, 1989
Tony Sellari (Design)
Ricardo Betancourt (Photo)

15 JAN

* Jan 16th, 1979
Aaliya Dana Haughton
Brooklyn (New York City)

Aaliyah
Try Again
Background Entertainment, 2000
Cover Artists Unknown

16 JAN

Athletic Progession
HHV, 2020
Rasmus Johansen (Design)
Mason London (Illustration)

17 JAN

Black Sheep
Flavor Of The Month
Mercury, 1991
Dana Brandwein (Design)
Alli Truch (Photo)

18 JAN

VENICE ANDERSON .PAAK

Anderson.Paak
Venice
Steel Wool Records, 2015
Dewey Saunders (Design)
Mike Dempsey (Photo)

19 JAN

T La Rock & Jazzy Jay
It's Yours
Partytime Records, 1984
Rick Rubin (Design)

20 JAN

CALVIN VALENTINE • PLUSH SEATS

プラツ天の座席

Calvin Valentine
Plush Seats
Mello Music Group, 2018
Cover Artists Unknown

21 JAN

* Jan 22nd, 1965
Jeffrey Allen Townes
Philadelphia (Pennsylvania)

DJ Jazzy Jeff
The Magnificent EP
Raster Records, 2002
Thomas 'Badshoes' Mc Callion (Design)
Mike Diver (Photo)

22 JAN

Mass Influence
Analyze / All Out
All Roght Fresh, 2020
H. Graphiks (Illustration)

23 JAN

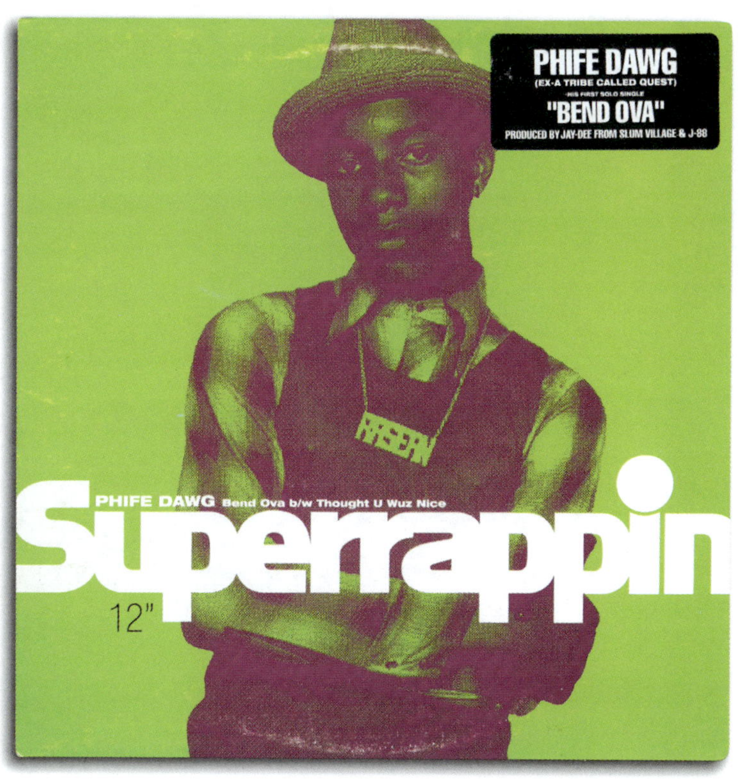

Superrappin – Phife Dwag
Bend Ova / Thought U Wuz Nice
Groove Attack Productions, 1999
Koeln80 (Design)

24 JAN

A Tribe Called Quest
Check The Rhime
Jive, 1991
ZombArt NG (Design)
Joe Grant (Photo)

25 JAN

Funkdoobiest
Bow Wow Wow
Epic, 1993
Dante Ariola, Jay Papke (Design)
Glenn Barr (Illustration)

26 JAN

Kinderzimmer Productions
Wir sind da wo oben ist
Virgin, 2002
Kathrin Hauser (Design)

27 JAN

Stereo MC's
33 45 78
4th & Broadway, 1989
Bite it! (Design)

28 JAN

Various Artists
Gangster Music Vol. 1
All City Records, 2019
bot.graphics (Design)
Gangster Doodles (Illustration)

29 JAN

Brand Nubian
Slow Down
Elektra, 1991
Cover Artists Unknown

30 JAN

* Jan 31st, 1981
Justin Randall Timberlake
Memphis (Tennessee)

Justin Timberlake
Like I Love You
Jive, 2002
Cover Artists Unknown

31 JAN

Beastie Boys
To The Five Boroughs
Capitol Records, 2004
Matteo Pericoli (Illustration)

01 FEB

L.A. Star
Poetess
Profile Records, 1990
Janet Perr (Design)
Caroline Greyshock (Photo)

Shuko & F Of Audiotreats
Cookies & Cream 4
For the Love of it, 2017
Cover Artists Unknown

03 FEB

True Love
I'm Bustin' Out
Critique, 1988
Cover Artists Unknown

04 FEB

Promoe
Off The Record
Street Level Record, 1999
Cover Artists Unknown

05 FEB

Deine Freunde
Helikopter
Sturmfreie Bude, 2019
Typeholics (Design)
Benjamin Kakrow (Illustration)

J Dilla
The Shining
EP2

* Feb 7th, 1974
James Dewitt Yancey
Detroit, Michigan (USA)

J Dilla
The Shining EP2
BBE, 2006
Jake Hollowoy (Design)

07 FEB

* Feb 8th, 1986
Brandon Paak Anderson
Oxnard (California)

Anderson.Paak
Come Down feat. T.I. / Room In Here
Steel Wool Records, 2016
Cover Artists Unknown

08 FEB

Majors
City Hall Records, 2008
Cover Artists Unknown

EPMD feat. L.L. Cool J
Rampage
Def Jam Recordings, 1991
Cover Artists Unknown

10 FEB

The Roots
Illadelph Halflife
DGC, 1996
Emily-Kate Berger, Julius L. Niskey (Design)
Michael Lavine (Photo)

11 FEB

Sir Mix-A-Lot
Baby Got Back
Def Jam Recordings, 1992
Dirk Walter (Design)
Mark Hanauer (Photo)

12 FEB

Artifacts
Wrong Side Of Da Tracks
Big Beat, 1994
Pawn Shop Press (Design)
Chi Mo Du, Martha Cooper, Pawn Shop Press (Photo)

13 FEB

* Feb 14th, 1972
Kendrick Jeru Davis
Brooklyn (New York City)

Jeru The Damaja
Come Clean
Payday, 1993
Peace Pype (Design)
Chi Modu (Photo)

14 FEB

MC Sway & DJ King Tech
Follow 4 Now / Time 4 Peace
All City Records, 1990
Bluewater Advertising & Design (Design)
Rick Martin (Illustration)

15 FEB

Kaos
"Court's In Session"
Bad Boy Records, 1988
Meddling Mendel (Design)
Richard Merchan (Illustration)

16 FEB

Greentea Peng
Man Made
AMF Records, 2021
Cover Artists Unknown

17 FEB

* Feb 18th, 1965
André Romell Young as Dr. Dre
Compton (California)

Obie Trice
The Set Up (You Don't Know)
Shady Records, 2004
Cover Artists Unknown

18 FEB

* Feb 19th, 1970
Robert Hall
Bronx (New York City)

Lord Finesse
The Awakening
Penalty Recordings, 1995
Sandy Lawrence (Design)
MoB (Photo)

19 FEB

Mos Def featuring Q-Tip & Tash
The Lyricist Lounge Vol. 1 Presents: Body Rock
Rawkus, 1998
Nobody Creative (Design)
Ge-ology / Gerard Young (Illustration)

20 FEB

Nu-Sounds
Mackin'
UNI Records, 1989
Janet Perr (Design)
Chris Carroll (Photo)

21 FEB

No Remorze
Condemned To Death On Da Day Da Lites Went Out
Buback, 1993
Fox 40, Uno (Photo)

22 FEB

* Feb 23rd, 1994
Simbiatu Abisola Abiola
Islington (London)

Little Simz
Sometimes I Might Be Introvert
Age 101 Music, 2021
Cover Artists Unknown

23 FEB

Original Soundtrack
(Music From The) Do The Right Thing
Motown, 1989
Jeff Adamoff (Design)

24 FEB

Big Shug
Crush
Payday, 1996
Stella Magloire (Design)
Gregory Burke (Photo)

25 FEB

Puppetmastaz
Creature Shock Radio
Louisville Records, 2005
Artificial Duck Flavour (Design)
Magnus Winter (Photo)

26 FEB

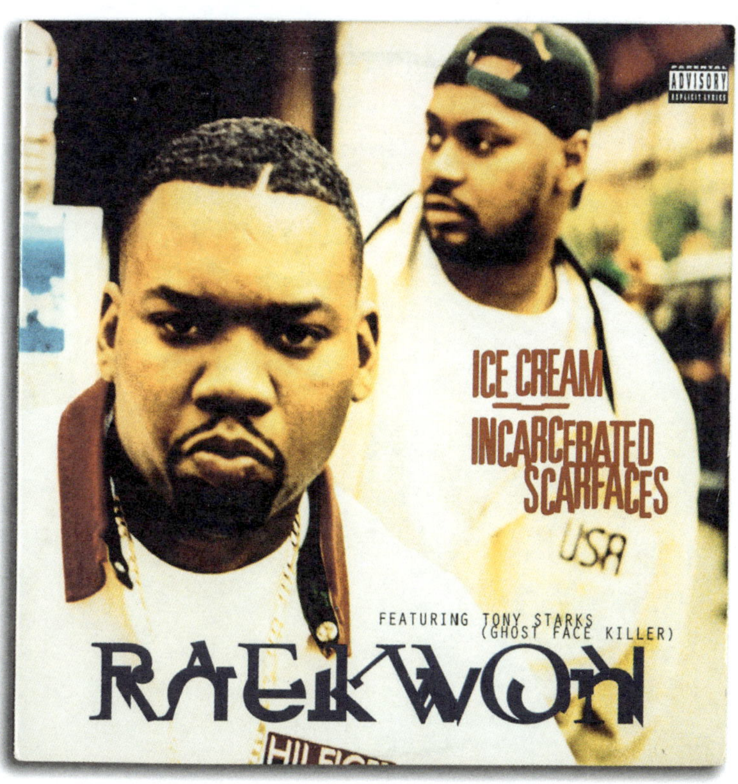

Raekwon
Ice Cream / Incarcerated Scarfaces
Loud Records, 1995
Miguel Rivera (Design)
Daniel Hastings (Photo)

27 FEB

Delinquent Habits
Tres Delinquentes
RCA, 1996
Thellus Singleton (Design)

28 FEB

Eric B. & Rakim
Juice (Know The Ledge)
MCA Records, 1992
Cover Artists Unknown

29 FEB

Co Real Artists
What About You (In The World Today)
Stones Throw Records, 2002
Cover Artists Unknown

01 MAR

Flying Lotus
Flamagra
Warp Records, 2019
Winston Hacking (Design)

02 MAR

TONE-LŌC

FUNKY COLD MEDINA

* Mar 3rd, 1966
Anthony Terrell Smith
Los Angeles (California)

Tone-Lōc
Funky Cold Medina
Island Records, 1989
Eric Haze (Design)

03 MAR

The 45 King & Louie Louie
Rhythmical Madness
Tuff City, 1989
Joey Vega (Illustration)

04 MAR

* Mar 5th, 1969
Claude M'Barali
Dakar (Senegal)

Mc Solaar
Caroline
Polydor, 1992
Alain Frappier (Design)
Philippe Bordas (Photo)

05 MAR

* Mar 6th, 1991
Tyler Gregory Okonma
Los Angeles (California)

Tyler, The Creator
Call Me If You Get Lost
Columbia, 2022
Gregory Ferrand (Design)

06 MAR

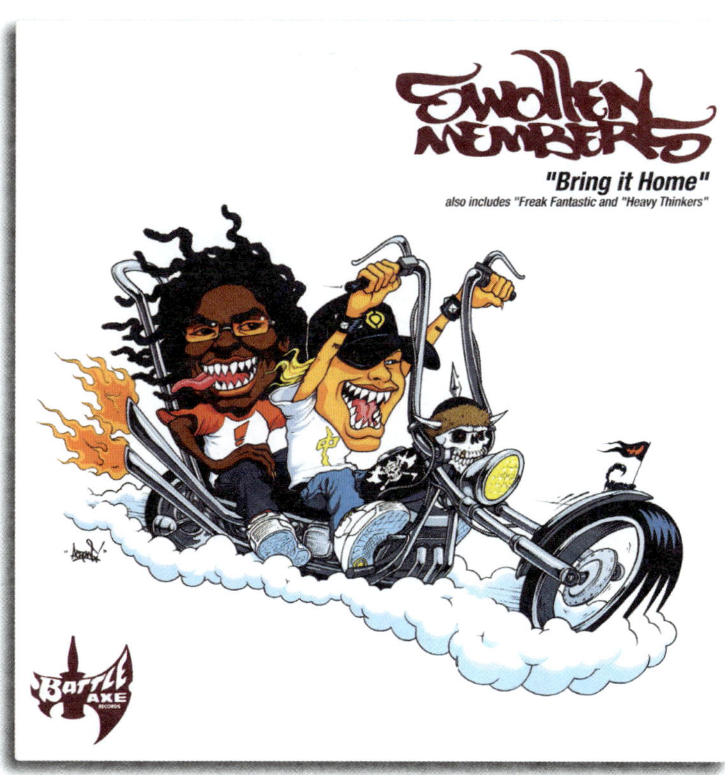

Swollen Members
Bring It Home
Battle Axe Records, 2002
Acrow (Illustration)

07 MAR

Various Artists
Mr. Magic's Rap Attack Volume 3
Profile Records, 1987
Harold Sinclair (Photo)

08 MAR

* Mar 9th, 1997
Christopher George Latore Wallace
Los Angeles (California)

The Notourious B.I.G Feat. Puff Daddy & Mase
Mo Money Mo Problems
Bad Boy Entertainment, 1997
Stereotype (Design)
Michael Lavine (Photo)

09 MAR

Reflection Eternal
Fortified Live / 2000 Seasons
Rawkus, 1997
Tim Ronan (Design)
Mrs. Mos Def (Photo)

10 MAR

Silvan Strauss
Facing
Kabul Fire, 2022
Marius Stepanek (Design)
Firas Colin (Illustration)

11 MAR

† Mar 12th, 2018
Craig Jamieson Mack
Walterboro (South Carolina)

Craick Mack
Mack Come Thru
Freeze Records, 2000
Cover Artists Unknown

12 MAR

The Nextmen
Spin It Round
Fat City, 2005
Cover Artists Unknown

13 MAR

Tom Misch & Yussef Dayes
What Kinda Music
Blue Note, 2020
Matt de Jong, Simone Cihlar (Design)

14 MAR

* Mar 15th, 1975
William James Adams Jr.
Los Angeles (California)

Will.I.Am
Lost Change (Original Soundtrack)
BBE, 2001
Thomas 'Badshoes' Mc Callion (Design)
Albert Watson (Photo)

15 MAR

Red Fox
Ghetto Gospel
Elektra, 1993
Cover Artists Unknown

* Mar 17th, 1927
Rudy Ray Moore
Fort Smith (Arkansas)

Rudy Ray Moore
The Third Rudy Ray Moore Album – The Cockpit
Kent, 1971
Ralph Pierce (Design)
Gladys Allen (Photo)

17 MAR

J.J. Fad
Supersonic (Remix)
Dream Team Records, 1988
Cover Artists Unknown

18 MAR

Texta
Nichts dagegen, aber
Tonträger Records, 2016
Johannes Mrazek (Design)
Gerhard Haderer (Illustration)

19 MAR

DJ KOOL

DJ KOOL

LET ME CLEAR MY THROAT

* Mar 20th, 1958
John W. Bowman
Washington DC (USA)

DJ Kool
Let Me Clear My Throat
American Recordings, 1996
Cover Artists Unknown

20 MAR

* Mar 21st, 1972
William Paul Mitchell
New York City (USA)

Large Professor
Radioactive
Matador, 2002
Cover Artists Unknown

21 MAR

Kings Of Swing
Nod Your Head To This / Go Cocoa!
Virgin, 1990
Steve J. Gerdes (Design)
Rocky Schenk (Photo)

22 MAR

Agallah
The Crookie Monster
Game Recordings, 1999
Todd "Dollars" James (Design)
Michael Benabib (Photo)

23 MAR

Original Soundtrack
Boyz N The Hood
Warner Bros. Records, 1991
Cover Artists Unknown

24 MAR

Lord Tariq & Peter Gunz
Deja Vu (Uptown Baby)
Columbia, 1997
Cover Artists Unknown

25 MAR

Lyrics Born
Callin' Out
Quannum Projects, 2003
Soap Design Co., LA (Design)
Grubby (Photo)

26 MAR

Deichkind
Noch fünf Minuten Mutti
Showdown, 2002
Dietmar Theis (Photo)

27 MAR

Black Moon
Buck Em Dow
Wreck Records, 1994
Chi Modu (Photo)

28 MAR

Eric B. & Rakim
In The Ghetto
MCA Records, 1990
Cesar Vera (Photo)

29 MAR

Various Artists
Battle Rock
X-Records, 1996
Mr. Boogie Cooke (Illustration)

30 MAR

Various Artists
The Rap Pack
Fresh Records, 1987
Meddling Mendel (Design)
Isaiah Roberts (Illustration)

31 MAR

Original Concept
Straight From The Basement Of Kooley High!
Def Jam Recordings, 1988
Steve Byram (Design)
Felix Unger (Photo)

01 APR

Create & Devastate
The Hitman / Just Get Down
Threshold Recordings, 2006
Cover Artists Unknown

02 APR

Outkast
Elevators (Me & You)
LaFace Records, 1996
D.L. Warfield (Design)
Tony Gaddis (Illustration)

03 APR

Dead Prez
It's Bigger Than Hip-Hop
Loud Records, 1999
Cover Artists Unknown

04 APR

Chunky A
Large And In Charge
MCA Records, 1989
Cover Artists Unknown

05 APR

Various Artists
Nothing To Lose – Music From Inspired By The Motion Picture
Tommy Boy, 1997
Cover Artists Unknown

06 APR

Fugees
The Score
Columbia, 1996
Brain (Design)
Marc Baptiste (Photo)

07 APR

* Apr 8th, 1964
Marcel Theo Hall
New York City (USA)

Biz Markie
Just A Friend
Cold Chillin', 1989
George DuBose (Design)

08 APR

Apollo Brown & Joell Ortiz
Mona Lisa
Mello Music Group, 2018
Austin Hart (Design)
Joey Dion (Photo)

09 APR

Suff Daddy
Basically Sober
Jakarta Records, 2022
Robert Winter (Design)
Andreas Samesson (Illustration)

10 APR

Blk Odyssy
Blk Vintage
Not on Label, 2022
Cover Artists Unknown

11 APR

MASTA ACE INCORPORATED

Born to Roll

* Apr 12th, 1967
Ulpiano Sergio Reyes
Pinar del Rio (Cuba)

Masta Ace Incorporated
Born To Roll
Delicious Vinyl, 1994
Cover Artists Unknown

12 APR

Royal Flush
World Wide
Blunt Recordings, 1996
Greg Knoll (Design)
Daniel Hastings (Photo)

13 APR

Blitz Mob
Blitz Vinyl, 1993
Ralf Kotthoff (Design)
Joachim „Bin Schon…" Rick (Illustration)

14 APR

Harmonic 33
Kaleidoscopic Sounds E.P.
Alphabet Zoo, 2001
Lee Framer (Design)

15 APR

Ganxsta Rid & The Otha Side
Occupation Hazardous
Bullet Proof Records, 1995
Cover Artists Unknown

16 APR

Naughty By Nature
O.P.P. / Wickedest Man Alive
Tommy Boy, 1991
Mark Weinberg (Design)

17 APR

Mc Paul Barman
How Hard Is That? / Housemate Troubles
Matador, 2000
Garland Lyn (Design)
Andrew Jeffrey Wright (Photo)

18 APR

† Apr 19th, 2010
Keith Edward Elam
New York City (USA)

Guru
Jazzmatazz Volume: 1 – Deluxe Edition
Virgin, 2018
Cover Artists Unknown

19 APR

† Apr 20th, 1975
Michael Santiago Render
Atlanta (Georgia)

Killer Mike
A.D.I.D.A.S.
Columbia, 2003
Cover Artists Unknown

20 APR

Ozomatli
Cut Chemist Suite
Almo Sounds, 1999
Cover Artists Unknown

21 APR

L'Orange X Jeremiah Jae
Complicate Your Life With Violence
Mello Music Group, 2019
David Lapham (Design)
Ruff Mercy (Illustration)

22 APR

Brothers Keepers
Adriano (Letzte Warnung)
Nitty Gritty Music, 2001
Cover Artists Unknown

23 APR

Boogie Down Productions
Jack Of Spades / I'm Still #1
Jive, 1988
Pietro Alfieri (Design)
Doug Rowell (Photo)

24 APR

Marsimoto
Green Juice
Green Berlin, 2015
zentraleberlin.com (Design)
Paul Ripke (Photo)

25 APR

Positively Black
Trumpet, 1989
Amy Bennick (Design)
Peter Bodtke (Photo)

Dynamite Deluxe
Wir Jetzt/Milestone
Eimsbush, 2000
KK1 // Typeholics (Design)
Gulliver Theis (Photo)

27 APR

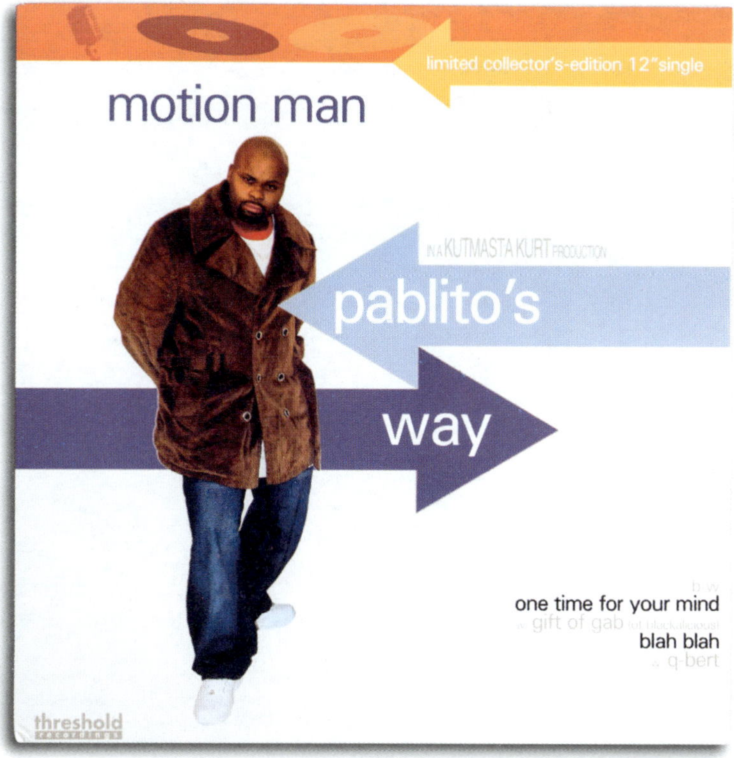

Motion Man
Pablito's Way
Threshold Recordings, 2006
Andy (Design)
D-Ray Archer (Photo)

28 APR

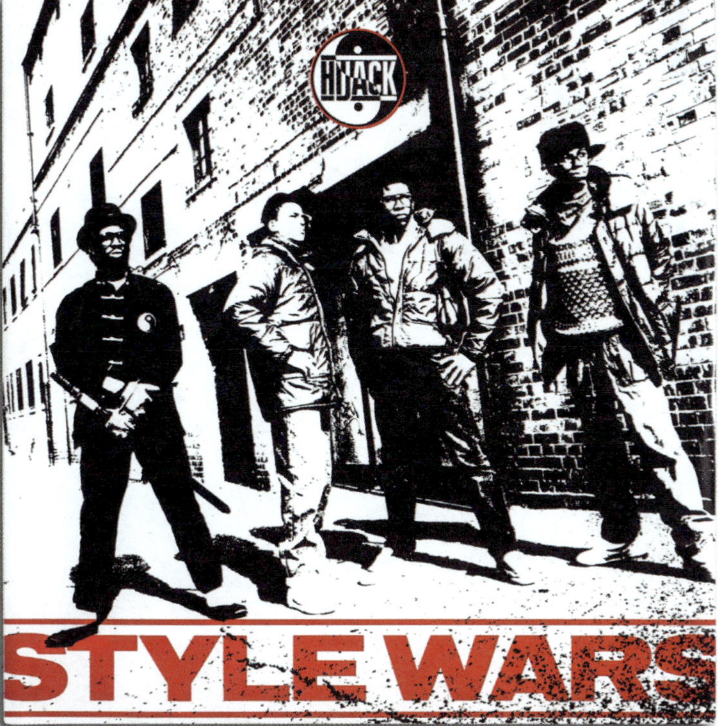

Hijack
Style Wars
Music of Life, 1988
Cover Artists Unknown

29 APR

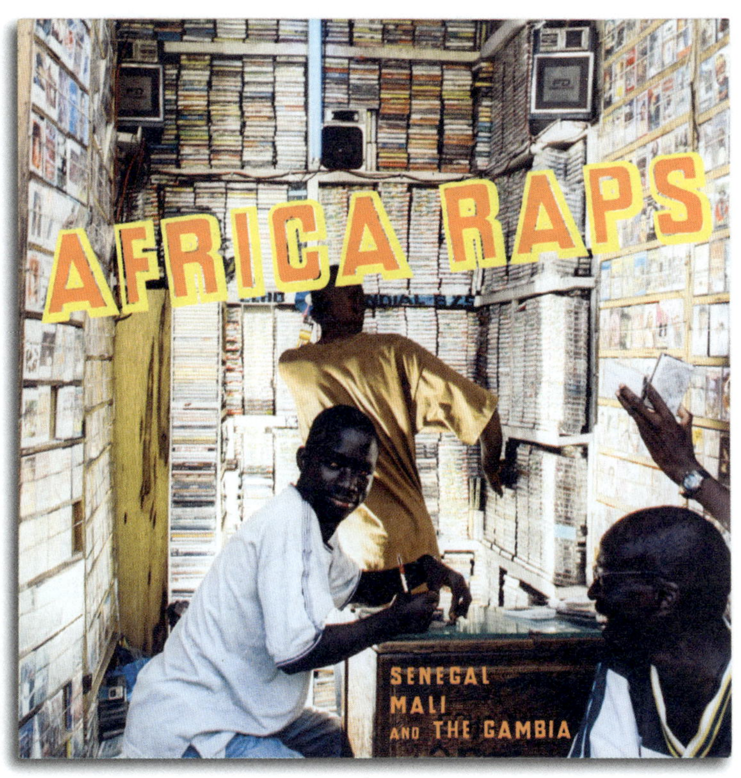

Various Artists
Africa Raps
Trikont, 2002
Hias Schaschko (Design)
Mark Janssen (Photo)

30 APR

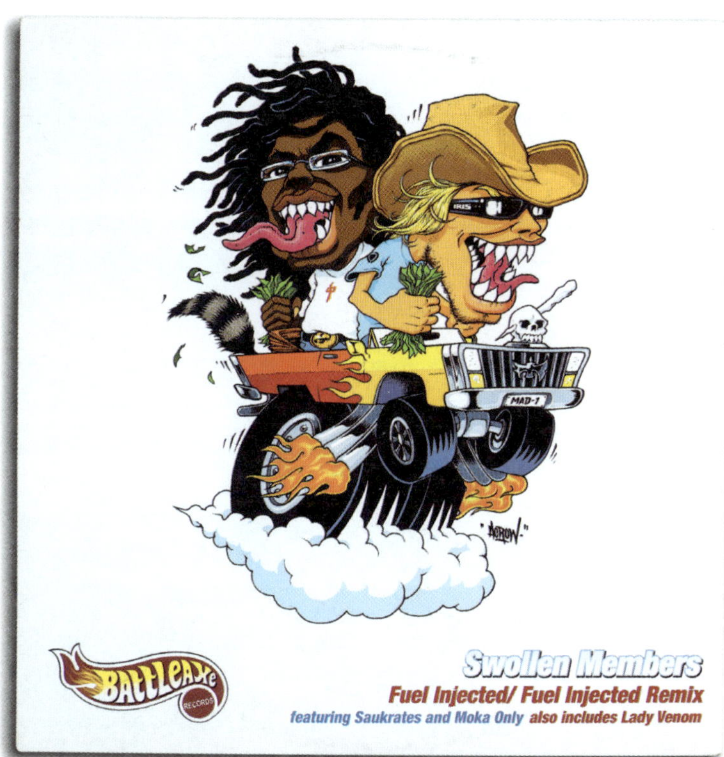

Swollen Members Feat. Saukrates & Moka Only
Fuel Injected / Fuel Injected Remix
Battle Axe Records, 2002
Path VCR (Design)
Acrow (Illustration)

01 MAY

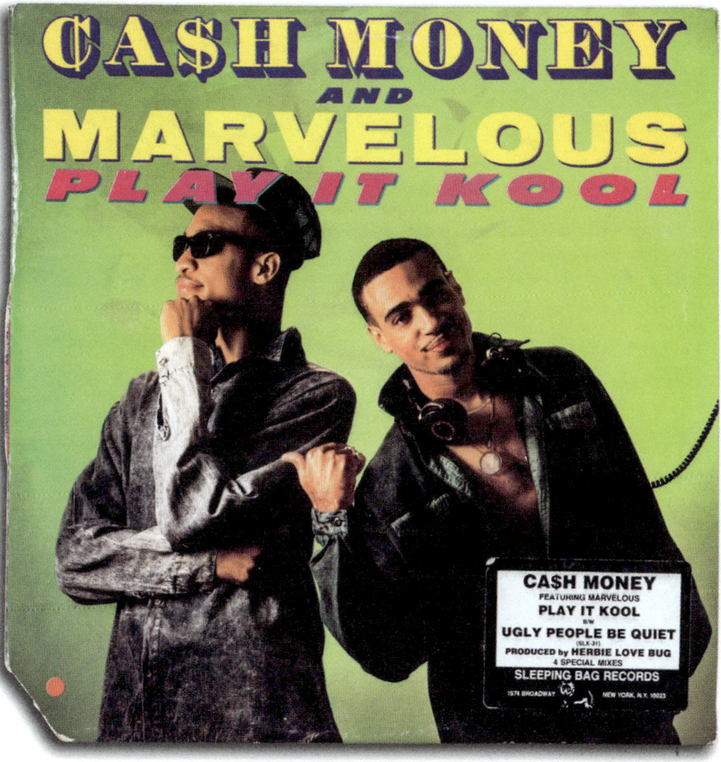

Ca$H Money And Marvelous
Play It Kool / Ugly People Be Quiet
Sleeping Bag Records, 1987
Icon Design (Design)
Frank Lindner (Photo)

02 MAY

PHAROAHE MONCH
SIMON SAYS
THE REMIXES
FEATURING REDMAN
METHOD MAN
SHABAAM SAHDEEQ
ROOTS MANUVA
SKITZ RODNEY P
RAWKUS

Pharoahe Monch
Simon Says (The Remixes)
Rawkus, 1999
Nobody (Design)
Franck Khalfoun (Photo)

03 MAY

Cus
Geballte Ladung
Blitz Vinyl, 1994
Illegal Overflow (Design)

04 MAY

A Tribe Called Quest
A Tribe Called Quest EP
Jive, 1994
Cover Artists Unknown

05 MAY

The High & Mighty Featuring Mos Def, El-P & Mike Zoot
B-Boy Document / Mind, Soul & Body
Eastern Conference, 1998
Cover Artists Unknown

06 MAY

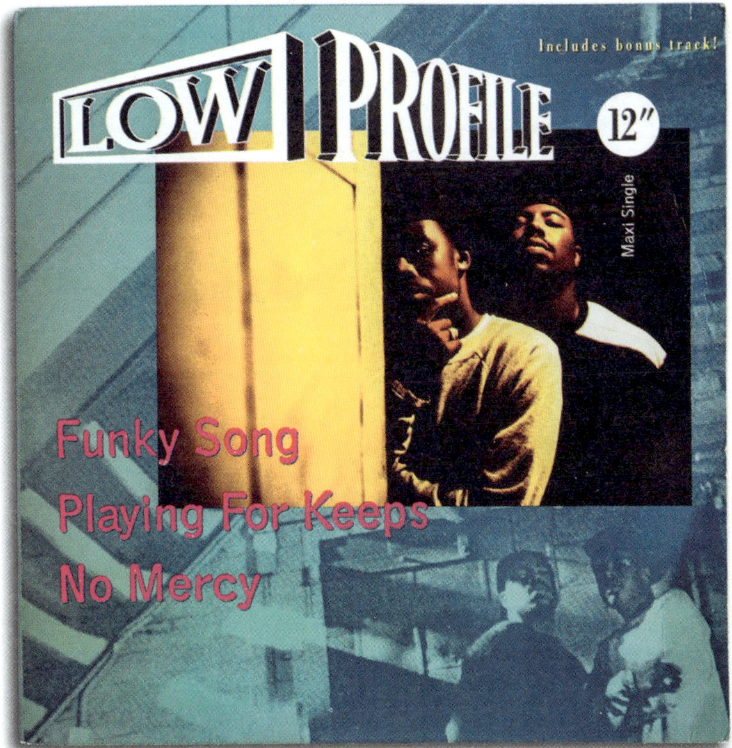

Low Profile
Funky Song / Playing For Keeps / No Mercy
Priority Records, 1990
Cover Artists Unknown

07 MAY

De La Soul
Ring Ring Ring (Ha Ha Hey)
Big Life, 1991
Mark Weinberg (Design)
Joseph Buckingham (Illustration)

08 MAY

Original Soundtrack
Straight Outta Compton
UMe, 2016
Howard Kim (Design)

09 MAY

* May 10th, 1967
Marvin Young
London (UK)

Young MC
Bust A Move
Island Records, 1988
Eric Haze (Design)
Salomon (Photo)

10 MAY

Various Artists
Mr. Magic's Rap Attack
Profile Records, 1985
Cover Artists Unknown

11 MAY

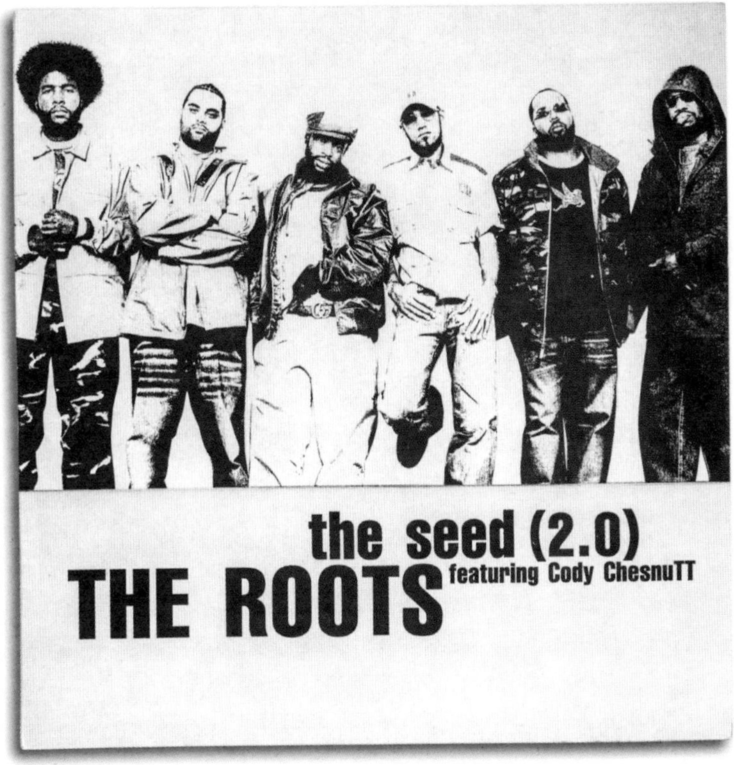

the seed (2.0)
THE ROOTS featuring Cody ChesnuTT

The Roots Featuring Cody Chesnutt
The Seed (2.0)
MCST, 2003
Cover Artists Unknown

12 MAY

Various Artists
Street Beat Volume II
Sugar Hill Records, 1984
Cover Artists Unknown

13 MAY

Jellybean
Wotupski!?!
EMI America, 1984
Henry Marquez (Design)
Duster, Seen (Illustration)

14 MAY

Cypress Hill
The Phuncky Feel One / How I Could Just Kill A Man
Ruffhouse Records, 1991
Cover Artists Unknown

15 MAY

* May 16th, 1966
Janet Damita Jo Jackson
Gary (Indiana)

Janet Jackson Featuring Q-Tip And Joni Mitchell
Got Til It's Gone
Virgin, 1997
Eddie Wolfl (Photo)

16 MAY

Lootpack

Weededed Remix
featuring Rasco and Oh No

plus

Loopdigga

feat. Medaphoar

Lootpack
Weededed Remix
Stones Throw Records, 2000
Cover Artists Unknown

The Cookie Crew
Born This Way
FFRR, 1989
Oscar Yong (Design)

18 MAY

Public Enemy
Muse Sick-N-Hour Mess Age
Def Jam Recordings, 1994
The Drawing Board (Design)
Mark Texeria (Illustration)

19 MAY

Various Artists
Break Mix
Metronome, 1984
Bobby (Design)
Jacques Sehy (Photo)

20 MAY

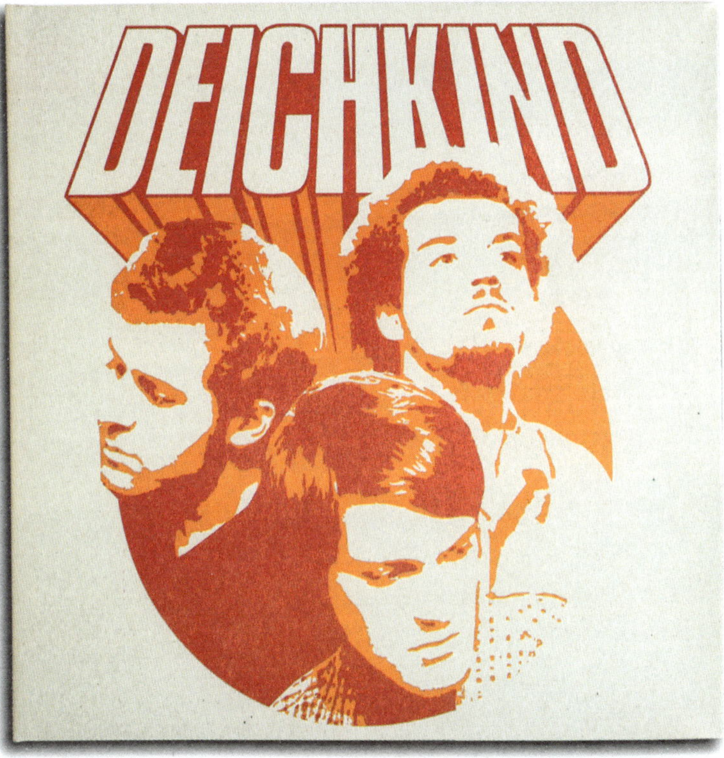

Deichkind
Bitte ziehen Sie durch
Showdown, 2000
Johannes Laue (Design)
Uli Heckmann (Photo)

21 MAY

La Boom
Atarihuana
Eimbush, 2002
Cover Artists Unknown

22 MAY

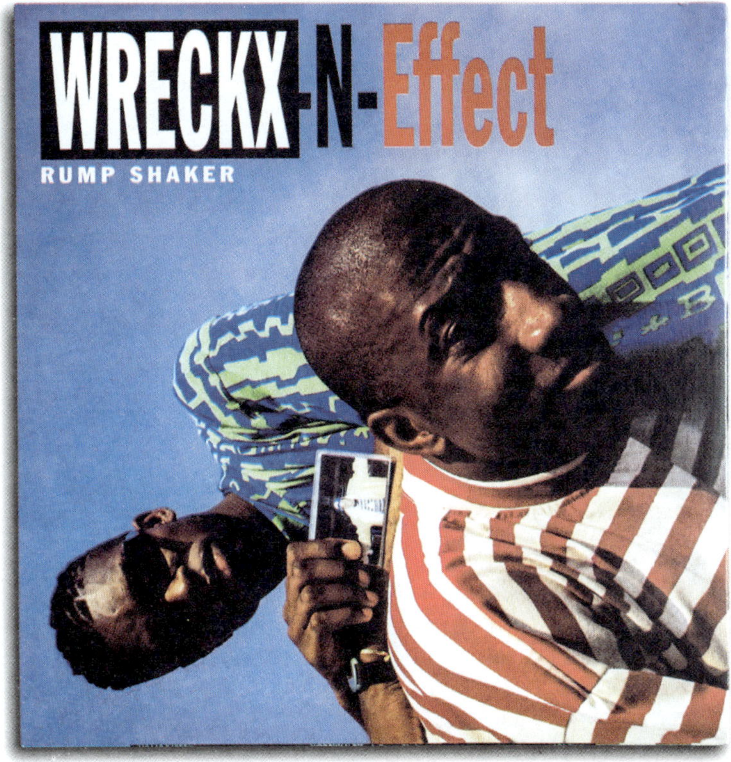

Wreckx-N-Effect
Rump Shaker
MCA Records, 1992
Cover Artists Unknown

23 MAY

Sad Night Dynamite
Parlophone Records Ltd, 2021
Alfie Dwyer (Design)
Angus Steele (Photo)

24 MAY

* May 25th, 1975
South Orange (New Jersey)

Lauryn Hill
Everything Is Everything
Columbia, 1999
Cover Artists Unknown

25 MAY

Tommy Tee
What's Your Name? / Above Da Law / Lethal Dosage
Tee Productions, 2001
Coderock@start.no (Design)

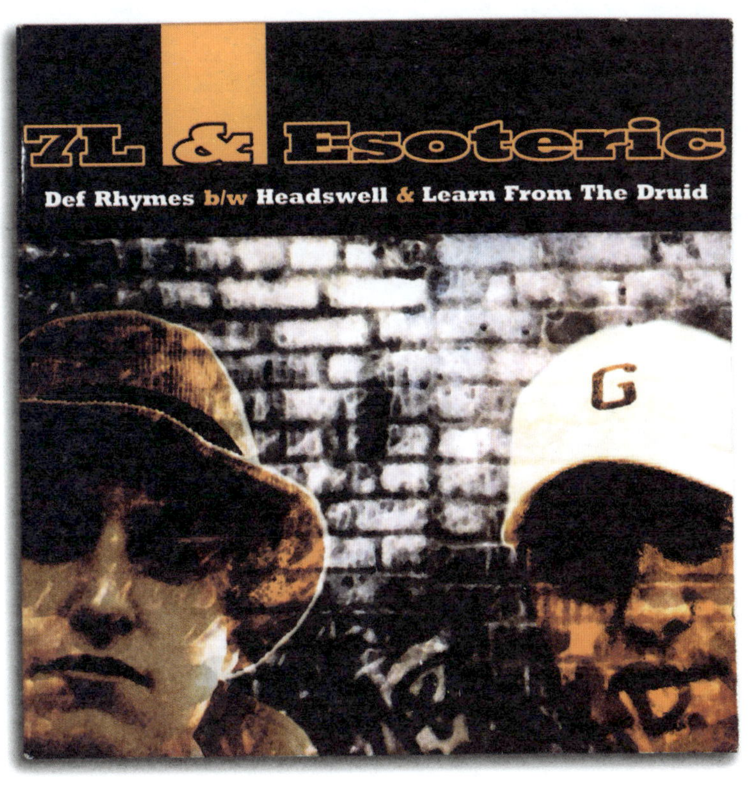

7L & Esoteric
Def Rhymes / Headswell / Learn From The Druid
Direct Records, 1998
Chino "Small But Strong" (Design)

27 MAY

Tha Alkaholiks
The Next Level
Loud Records, 1995
Natas Kaupas (Design)
Ricardo Martin (Photo)

28 MAY

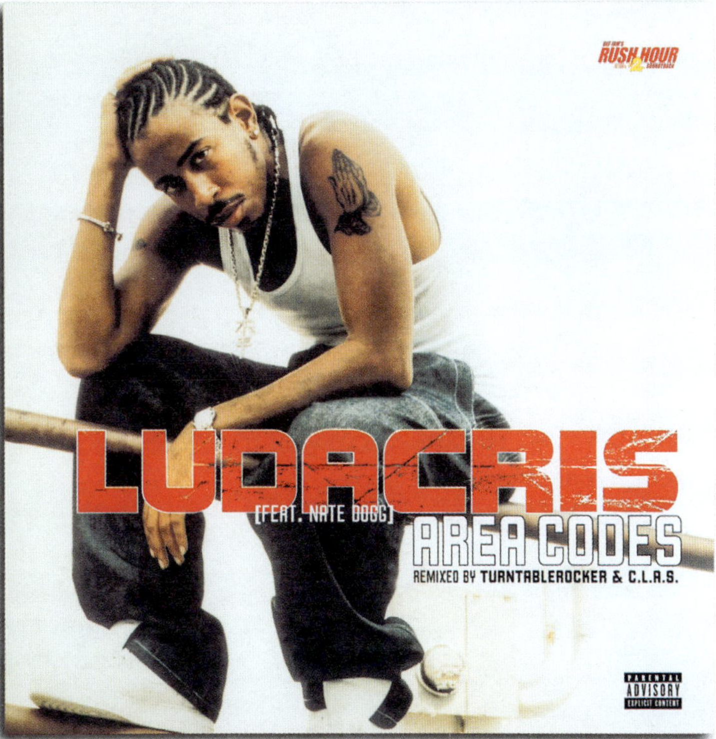

Ludacris
Area Codes
Def Jam South, 2001
Cover Artists Unknown

29 MAY

* May 30th, 1974
Lamont Coleman
Harlem (New York City)

Big L
Ebonics / Size 'Em Up
Flamboyant Entertainment, 1998
Ruben 'Jaz' Ortiz (Design)
Ricky Powell (Photo)

30 MAY

Advanced Chemistry
Dir fehlt der Funk!
Intercord Record Service, 1994
Grafik-Design-Studio Heidelberg (Design)
Stefan Berg (Photo)

31 MAY

ANTILOPEN GANG PRÄSENTIERT

danger dan

REFLEXIONEN AUS DEM BESCHÖNIGTEN LEBEN

* Jun 1st, 1983
Daniel Pongratz
Aachen (Germany)

Danger Dan
Reflexionen aus dem beschönigten Leben
Jochens Kleine Plattenfirma (JKP), 2018
Marcel "Maz" Richard (Design)

01 JUN

Cut Chemist
The Garden / Storm
A Stable Sound, 2006
Cover Artists Unknown

02 JUN

Readykill
Buback, 1993
Marcel "Maz" Richard, Hesh (Design)

03 JUN

Fettes Brot
Singt Rio Reiser: Ich bin müde
Safety Records, 2003
Cover Artists Unknown

04 JUN

Dilated Peoples
The Platform
ABB Records, 2000
Brent Rollins (Design)
Jana Taylor (Photo)

05 JUN

Blumentopf
Wir
Virgin, 2010
Cover Artists Unknown

06 JUN

Rag
Unter Tage
Put Da Needle To Da Records, 1998
Fast Forward, RAG (Design)
Astrid Milewski (Photo)

07 JUN

* Jun 8th, 1977
Kanye Omari West
Atlanta (Georgia)

Kanye West / Nas / KRS-One / Rakim
Better Than I've Ever Been
Nike, 2007
Cover Artists Unknown

08 JUN

Gone Fishing

FERGE X FISHERMAN

Ferge X Fisherman
Gone Fishing
Not On Label, 2018
Cover Artists Unknown

09 JUN

* Jun 10th, 1968
Tracy L. Curry
Houston (Texas)

The D.O.C.
It's Funky Enough / No One Can Do It Better
Ruthless Records, 1989
Cover Artists Unknown

10 JUN

PUBLIC ENEMY

NIGHT OF THE LIVING BASEHEADS

COLD LAMPIN' WITH FLAVOR
TERMINATOR X TO THE EDGE OF PANIC

Public Enemy
Night Of The Living Baseheads
Def Jam Recordings, 1988
Cover Artists Unknown

11 JUN

Cash Crew
Will It Make My Brown Eyes Blue?
Scream, 1991
Hills Archer Ink (Design)
Pete Ashworth (Photo)

12 JUN

Kool G Rap & DJ Polo
Road To The Riches
Cold Chillin', 1989
JoDee Stringham (Design)
George Du Bose (Photo)

13 JUN

* Jun 14th, 1969
Lorenzo Patterson
Copton (California)

MC Ren
Kizz My Black Azz
Ruthless Records, 1992
Dino Paredes (Design)
Dean Kerr (Photo)

* Jun 15th, 1969
O'Shea Jackson
Baldwin Hills (California)

Ice Cube
AmeriKKKa's Most Wanted
Priority Records, 1990
Kevin Hosmann (Design)
Mario Castellanos (Photo)

15 JUN

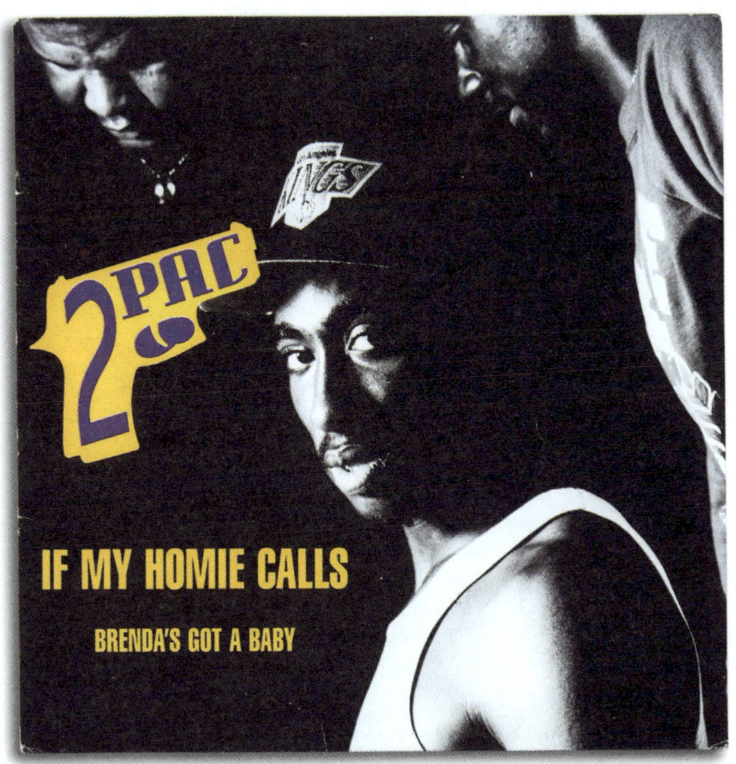

* Jun 16th, 1971
Tupac Amaru Shakur
Manhattan (New York City)

2Pac
If My Homie Calls / Brenda's Got A Baby
Interscope Records, 1992
Cover Artists Unknown

16 JUN

Tribez. X Maniac
Paragon (Tribez. Collection I)
Beat Art Department, 2020
Cover Artists Unknown

17 JUN

Kid 'N' Play
Gittin' Funky
Select Records, 1988
Cover Artists Unknown

18 JUN

CALL ME
D·NICE

* Jun 19th, 1970
Derrick T. Jones
New York City (USA)

D-Nice
Call Me D-Nice
Jive, 1990
Catanzaro & Mahdessian (Photo)

19 JUN

Prodigy
Keep It Thoro
Loud Records, 2000
Cover Artists Unknown

20 JUN

* Jun 21st, 1970
Peter Philipps
Mount Vernon (New York City)

Pete Rock
Petestrumentals 2
Mello Music Group, 2015
Jeremy Deputat (Photo)

21 JUN

Bass Patrol
Rock This Planet
Joey Boy Records, 1988
Cover Artists Unknown

22 JUN

Advanced Chemistry
Fremd im eigenen Land
MZEE Records, 1992
Ralf Kotthoff (Design)
Akim (Photo)

23 JUN

Just-Ice
Na Touch Da Just / Freedom Of Speech '88
Fresh Records, 1988
Icon Design (Design)
Janette Beckman (Photo)

24 JUN

Flashmaster Ray
Flashback
P.O.sin-Music, 2014
Cover Artists Unknown

25 JUN

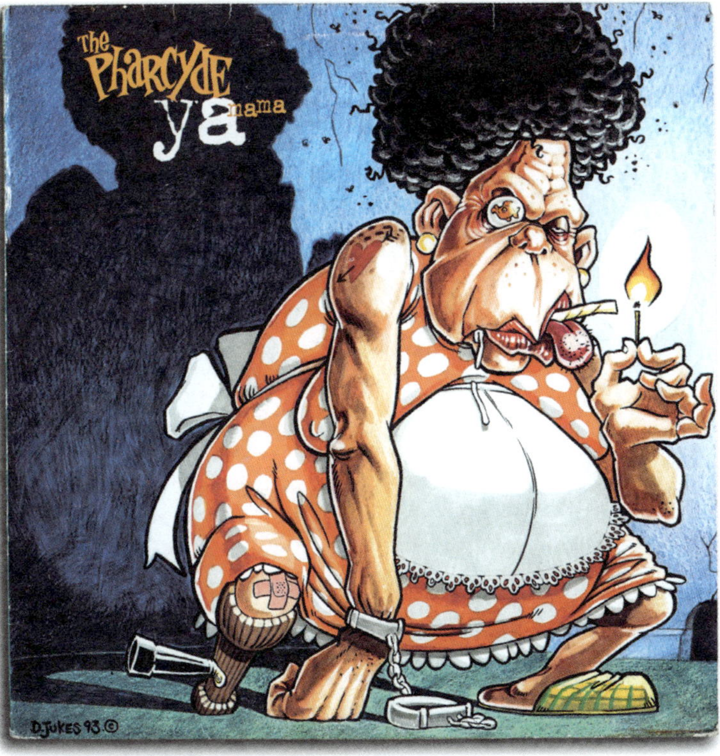

The Pharcyde
Ya Mama
Delicious Vinyl, 1993
Erik Brunetti (Illustration)

Dendemann
Das Schweigen Dilemma
Yo Mama's Recording, 2003
Edgar Walthert (Illustration)

27 JUN

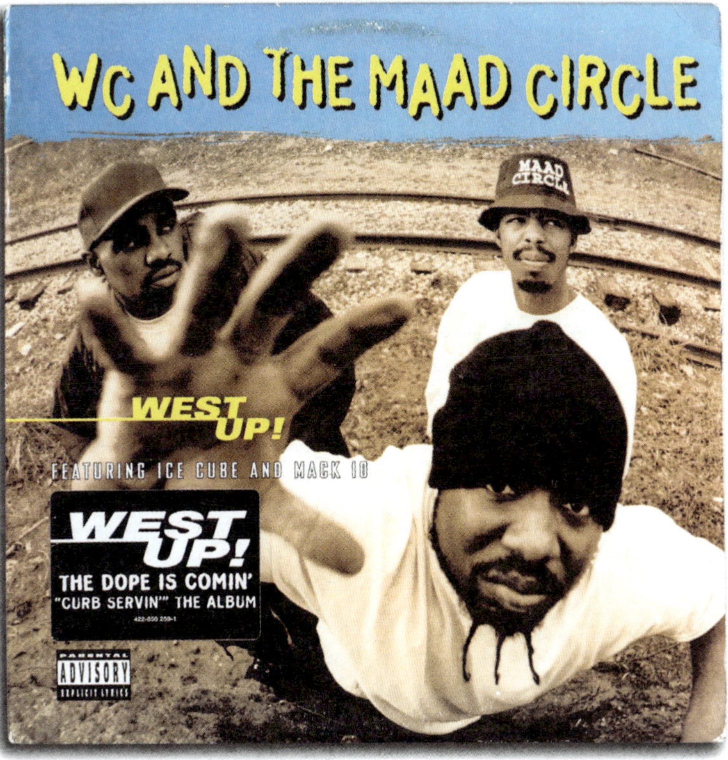

WC And The Maad Circle
West Up!
London Records, 1995
Edward O'Dowd (Design)
Leslie Sokolow (Photo)

28 JUN

* Jun 29th, 1972
Joshua Paul Davis
San José (California)

DJ Shadow
Our Pathetic Age
Mass Appeal, 2019
DJ Shadow (Design)
Michael Lukowski, Paul Insect (Illustration)

29 JUN

Various Artists
Schützt die Rille
Köln Massive, 1994
Pütz, Gadget, Markus Quarta, Paul Kalkbrenner (Design)
Illegal Overflow (Illustration)

30 JUN

* Jul 1st, 1971
Meliis Arnette "Missy" Elliott
Portsmouth (Virginia)

Missy Elliot
Under Construction
Elektra, 2002
Anita Marisa Boriboon (Design)
Jeff Reidel (Photo)

01 JUL

Kanye West
Stronger
Roc-A-Fella Records, 2007
Takashi Murakami (Illustration)

02 JUL

Kool Moe Dee
Funke Funke Wisdom
Jive, 1991
Sally Boon (Photo)

03 JUL

The Crash Crew / Funky Four
Crash Crew Meets Funky Four
Sugar Hill Records, 1983
X (Photo)

KINDERZIMMER PRODUCTIONS
TODESVERACHTUNG TO GO

Kinderzimmer Productions
Todesverachtung To Go
Grönland Records, 2020
Frank Schäfer (Design)

05 JUL

* Jul 6th, 1975
Curtis James Jackson III
Queens (New York City)

50 Cent
P.I.M.P.
Shady Records, 2003
Cover Artists Unknown

06 JUL

Poor Righteous Teachers
Holy Intellect / Self-Styled Wisdom
Profile Records, 1990
Rick Demann (Design)

07 JUL

L'Orange
The Ordinary Man
Mello Music Group, 2017
Drew Tetz (Illustration)

08 JUL

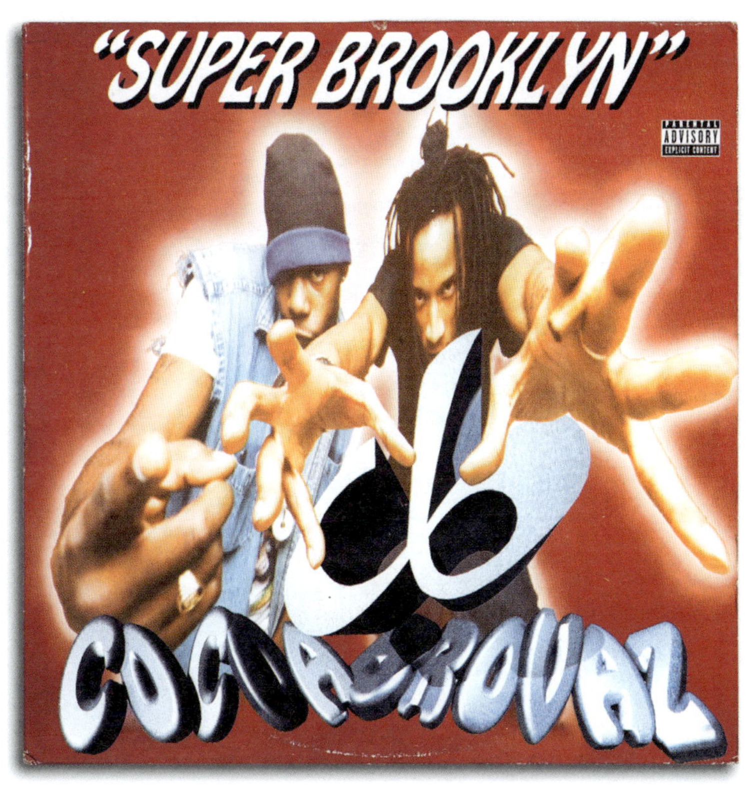

Cocoa Brovaz
Super Brooklyn
Duck Down, 2000
Rick Nucci (Design)

09 JUL

Various Artists
Pioniermanöver – Hip Hop aus der DDR
Halb 7 Records, 1994
Kretschi & Basti (Design)

10 JUL

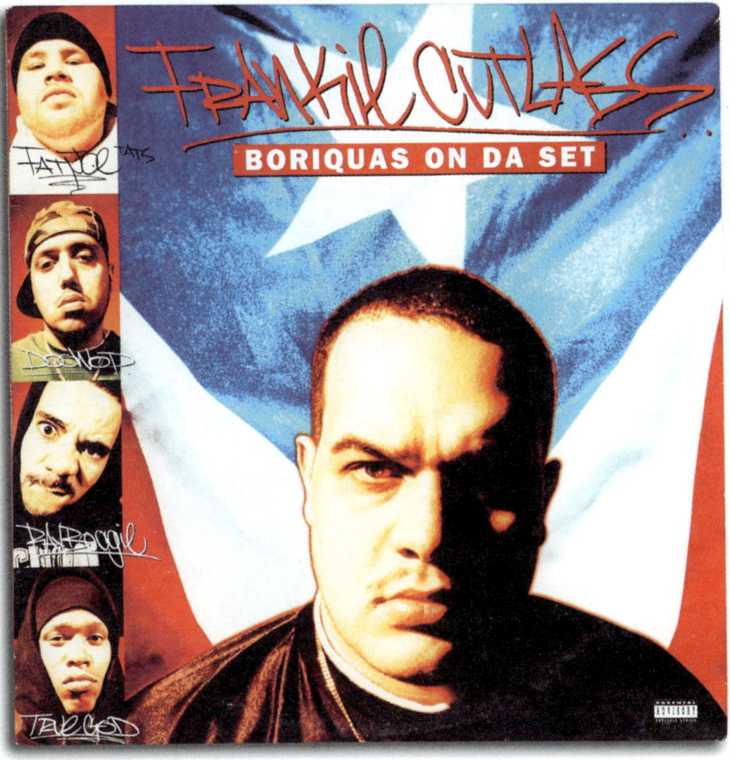

Frankie Cutlass
Boriquas On Da Set
Relativity, 1995
Cover Artists Unknown

11 JUL

Darth Fader & Scarecrow Willy
Toasted Marshmallow Feet Braxe
Dirt Style Records , 1995
Cover Artists Unknown

12 JUL

Noname
Room 25
Not On Label, 2022
Cover Artists Unknown

13 JUL

Beginner
Morgen Freeman
Buback, 2004
Typeholics (Design)
Eva Salzmann, Klaus Salzmann (Illustration)

14 JUL

Kuso Gvki
Culture
Block Opera, 2019
Cover Artists Unknown

15 JUL

DJ Adlib
Adlibertine
Alphabet Zoo, 2006
Cover Artists Unknown

16 JUL

* Jul 17th, 1961
Keith Edward Elam
Boston (Massachuetts)

Guru
Jazzmatazz Volume: 1
Chrysalis, 1993
Henry Marquez (Design)
Humphrey Studio (Photo)

17 JUL

Puppetmastaz
Humans Get All The Credit
New Noise, 2002
Mad Eye Berlin (Design)
Sim Gil (Photos)

18 JUL

The Roots
Don't Say Nuthin'
Geffen Records, 2004
Cover Artists Unknown

19 JUL

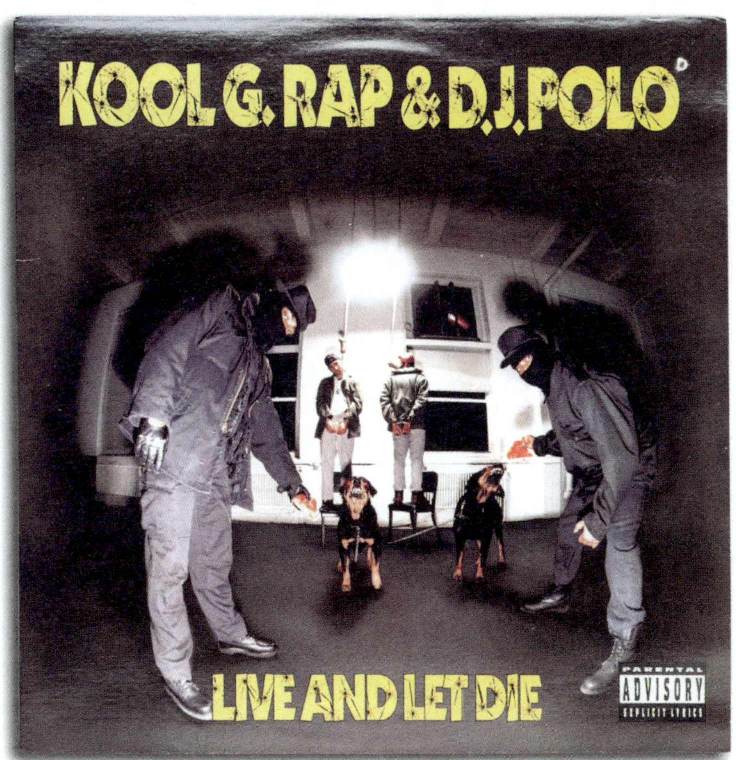

* Jul 20th, 1968
Nathaniel Wilson
Queens (New York City)

Kool G. Rap & D.J. Polo
Live And Let Die
Cold Chillin', 1992
Pop Eye Designs (Design)
George DuBose (Photo)

20 JUL

* Jul 21st, 1978
Damian Robert Nesta Marley
Kingston (Jamaica)

Damian Jr. Gong Marley
All Night Feat. Stephen Marley
Tuff Gong International, 2006
Cover Artists Unknown

21 JUL

Ultramagnetic MC's
Poppa Large
Mercury, 1992
Annette Cirillo (Design)
Michael Lavine (Photo)

22 JUL

The Pase Rock
Lindsay Lohan's Revenge
Fully Fitted, 2007
The Pase Rock (Design)
Pieter Janssen (Illustration)

23 JUL

The Last Poets
Chastisment
Blue Thumb Records, 1972
Jim Dyson (Illustration)

24 JUL

F.A.B.
Erich Privat
F.AT A.SS B.EATS, 1997
FUEGO / Friedel Muders (Design)
Gaby Gerster (Photo)

25 JUL

* Jul 26th, 1993
Michael Omari
London (UK)

Stormzy
Heavy Is The Head
Merky Records, 2020
Cover Artists Unknown

26 JUL

Common
One-Nine-Nine-Nine / Like They Used To Say
Rawkus, 1999
Jeff Staple (Design)
Mrs. Mos Def / Jeannie Bizé (Photo)

27 JUL

Eko Fresh
Jetzt kommen wir wieder auf die Sachen
German Dream Evangelium, 2009
Bastian Sobtzick (Illustration)

28 JUL

Boot Camp
Think Back
Duck Down, 2002
Cover Artists Unknown

29 JUL

Massive Töne
Überfall
EastWest, 1999
Elmar Jäger (Design)
Maja Müller (Photo)

30 JUL

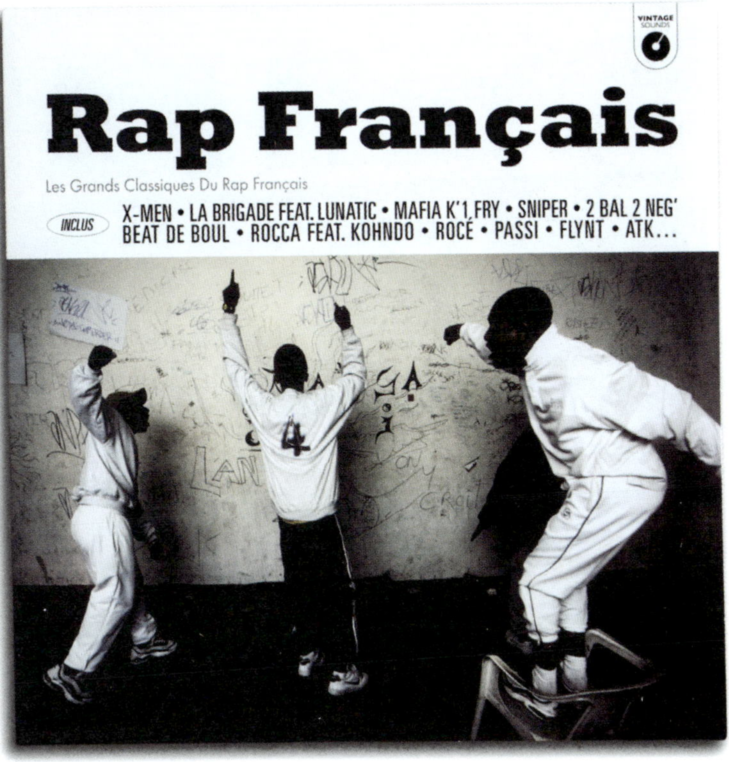

Rap Français

Les Grands Classiques Du Rap Français

X-MEN • LA BRIGADE FEAT. LUNATIC • MAFIA K'1 FRY • SNIPER • 2 BAL 2 NEG'
BEAT DE BOUL • ROCCA FEAT. KOHNDO • ROCÉ • PASSI • FLYNT • ATK...

Various Artists
Rap Français (Les Grands Classiques Du Rap Français)
Wagram Music, 2020
Supercinq (Design)
Jean-Erick Pasquier (Photo)

31 JUL

AFROB

beats, rhymes & mr. scarda-nelli

* Aug 1st, 1977
Robert Zemichiel
Unknown (Italy)

Afrob
Beats, Rhymes & Mr. Scardanelli
One Shotta Records, 2017
Dennis Dirksen (Design)
Georg Roske, Samon Kawamura (Photo)

01 AUG

Ty
Groovement / Ha Ha
Big Dada Recordings, 2003
25Survivorstudio (Design)
Tom Oldham (Photo)

DJ Format
Ill Culinary Behaviour
Genuine, 2001
Cover Artists Unknown

03 AUG

* Aug 4th, 1918
Robert Lee Maupin
Chicago (USA)

Iceberg Slim
Reflections
Ala, 1976
Jim Rasfeld (Design)
Robert Wotherspoon (Photo)

04 AUG

Walkin'Large
Reachin' (For My People...) / When I Flow
Groove Attack Productions, 1995
The Weusthoff & Rose Communication Bureau (Design)
Silke S. Kammann (Photo)

05 AUG

FLAKO
MESEKTET
TEN YEAR ANNIVERSARY EDITION

fLako
Mesektet Ten Year Anniversary Edition
Project: Mooncircle, 2021
Robert Winter (Photo)

06 AUG

Suprême NTM
Authentik
Epic, 1991
Cover Artists Unknown

07 AUG

* Aug 8th, 1962
Mohandes DeWese
Harlem (New York City)

Kool Moe Dee
Knowledge Is King
Jive, 1989
Pietro Alfieri (Design)
Douglas Rowell (Photo)

* Aug 9th, 1959
Kurtis Walker
Harlem (New York City)

Kurtis Blow
Back By Popular Demand
Mercury, 1988
Cover Artists Unknown

09 AUG

Oran Juice Jones Feat. Stu Large & Camp Lo
Poppin That Fly… (With Clark Kent Remixes)
Tommy Boy, 1997
Cover Artists Unknown

10 AUG

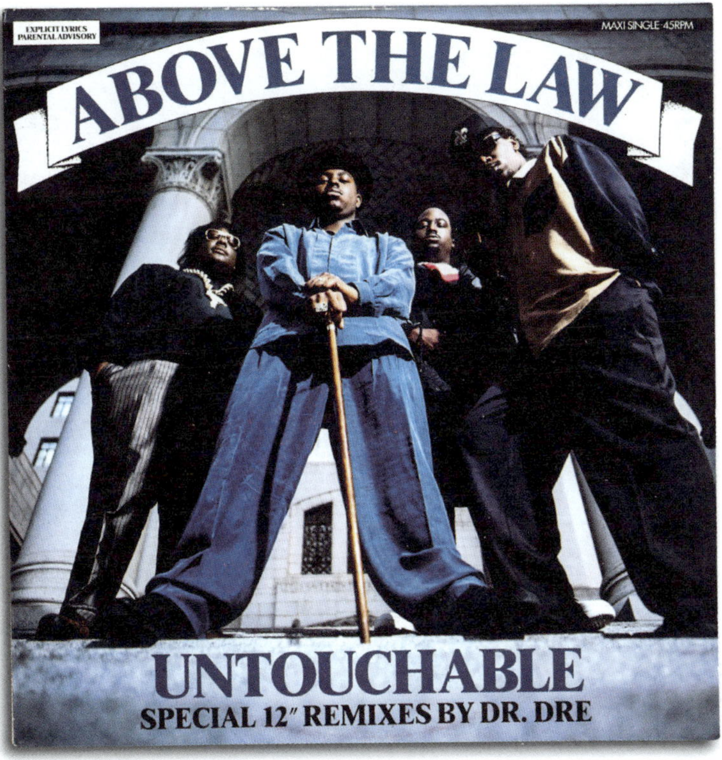

Above The Law
Untouchable
Epic, 1990
Helane Freeman (Design)
Peter Dokus (Photo)

11 AUG

Hurricane
The Hurra
Grand Royal, 1995
Olivier Carrié (Design)
Marina Chavez (Photo)

12 AUG

DJ Sat-One
Any Champion / Fuk Dat Shit
Readyrock Records, 1999
DJ Sat-One (Illustration)

13 AUG

MC ADE
How Much Can You Take
4 Sight Records, 1989
Associated Studios (Design)
Mark Hill (Photo)

14 AUG

Method Man
The Riddler
Atlantic, 1995
Cover Artists Unknown

15 AUG

Del! The Funky Homosapien
No Feed For Alarm
Elektra, 1993
Scott Idleman (Design)
Carl Posey (Photo)

16 AUG

Danny Breaks
The Outer Dimension
Alphabet Zoo, 2005
Lee Farmer (Design)
Helen Coombes (Photo)

17 AUG

Artifacts
The Ultimate
Big Beat, 1997
Cover Artists Unknown

18 AUG

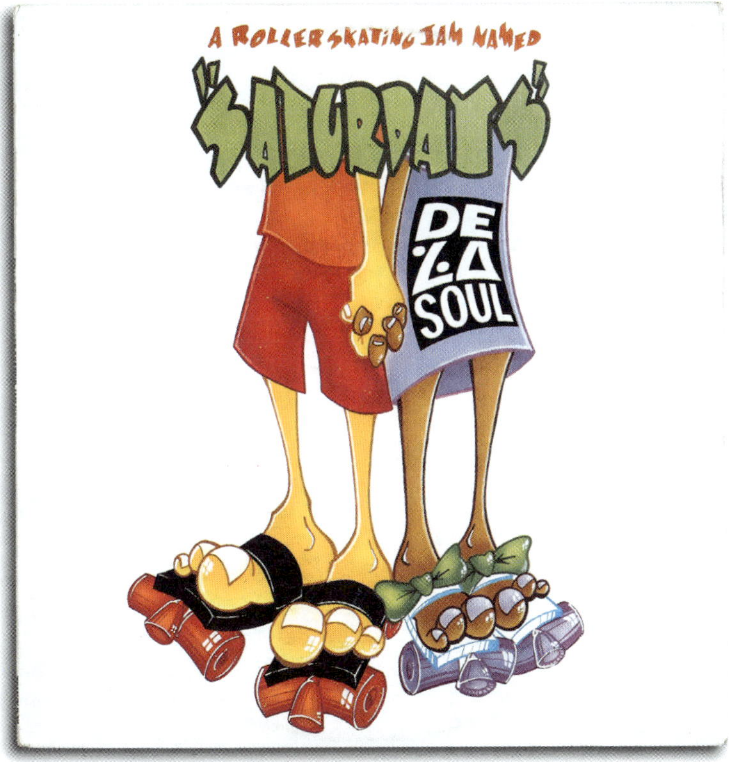

De La Soul
A Roller Skating Jam Named "Saturdays"
Tommy Boy, 1991
Mark Weinberg (Design)
Joseph Buckingham Jr. (Illustration)

19 AUG

· KRS ONE · STEP INTO A WORLD (RAPTURE'S DELIGHT)

* Aug 20th, 1965
Lawrence Parker
Park Slope (New York City)

KRS-One
Step Into A World (Rapture's Delight)
Jive, 1997
Alexander Maslatzides (Design)
Simone Allen (Photo)

20 AUG

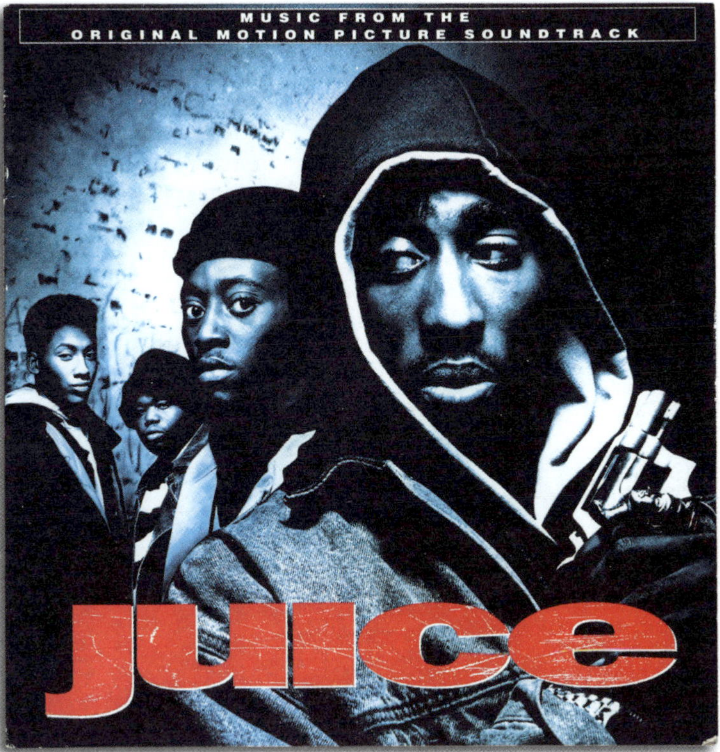

Original Soundtrack
Juice
Soul, 1992
Vartan (Design)
Adger W. Cowans (Photo)

21 AUG

* Aug 22nd, 1966
Gary Grice
Brooklyn (New York City)

Genius / GZA Feat. Inspektah Deck A.K.A Rollie Fingers
Cold World
Geffen Records, 1995
Cyril Gittens (Design)
Denys Cowans (Illustration)

22 AUG

Rudy Ray Moore
Close Encounter Of The Sex Kind
Generation International, 1978
Coop (Design)

23 AUG

Nightmares On Wax
Know My Name
Warp Records, 2002
Intro Design (Design)

24 AUG

* Aug 25th, 1973
Dwight Conroy Farrell
Bronx (New York City)

Count Bass-D
Pre-Life Crisis
Work, 1995
Michelle Willems (Design)
Eric Johnson (Photo)

25 AUG

DJ Hype feat. Souls of Mischief
Ubiquitous / Pull Out Your Cut (Remix)
Masters On Broadway, 2003
Cover Artists Unknown

26 AUG

Loyle Carner
Not Waving, But Drowning
AMF Records, 2019
Mauro Borges, Rory Dewar (Design)
French Vanilla (Photo)

27 AUG

Ugly Duckling
Turn It Up
Antidote, 2003
Jake Steel (Illustration)

28 AUG

T9
King Fu
OFDM, 2021
Johannes Brückner (Illustration)

29 AUG

Ultramagnetic M.C.'s
Make It Happen
Mercury, 1991
Alli Truch (Design)

30 AUG

Ludacris Featuring Pharrell Williams
Money Maker
Disturbing Tha Peace , 2006
Cover Artists Unknown

31 AUG

Kinderzimmer Productions
Die hohe Kunst der tiefen Schläge
Kinderzimmer Recordings, 1999
Karin Hauser (Design)

01 SEP

Big Daddy Kane
Taste Of Chocolate
Cold Chillin', 1990
George Du Bose (Photo)

Rock Da Most
Use The Posse EP
Imperial Nation Records, 1989
Cover Artists Unknown

03 SEP

* Sep 4th, 1973
Beyoncé Giselle Knowles-Carter
Houston (Texas)

Beyoncé
Crazy In Love
Columbia, 2003
Cover Artists Unknown

04 SEP

Anti Pop Consortium
What Am I?
75 Ark, 2000
Benitez/Del Sur (Design)

05 SEP

Stepchild
Hangin' Around (Sicka Gettin' Treated...)
Warner Bros. Records, 1995
Cover Artists Unknown

06 SEP

Demon Boyz
Recognition
Music Of Life, 1989
Norman Anderson (Photo)

07  SEP

RJD2
June
Def Jux, 2001
Cover Artists Unknown

08 SEP

DJ Serious
Popped
Audio Research Records, 2001
Eskimo Design, HeadlessHeroes (Design)

09 SEP

* Sep 10th, 1968
Antonio M. Hardy
Brooklyn (New York City)

Big Daddy Kane
Long Live The Kane
Cold Chillin', 1988
George DuBose (Photo)

10 SEP

Original Soundtrack
Battle Of The Year 2001
Def Jam Germany, 2001
Mode 2 (Design)

11 SEP

Elaquent
Forever Is A Pretty Long Time
Mello Music Group, 2020
Motel (Design)

12 SEP

* Sep 13th, 1974
Keith Murray
Brooklyn (New York City)

Keith Murray
The Most Beautifullest Thing In This World
Jive, 1994
Miguel Rivera (Design)
Daniel Hastings (Photo)

13 SEP

* Sep 14th, 1973
Nasir Bin Olu Dara Jones
Brooklyn (New York City)

Nas Feat. Olu Dara
Bridging The Gap
Columbia, 2004
Cover Artists Unknown

14 SEP

N*E*R*D
She Wants To Move
Virgin, 2004
Jane Morledge (Design)
Sasha Waldman (Photo)

15 SEP

* Sep 16th, 1961
Terrence Ronnie Keaton
Bronx (New York City)

T La Rock
Lyrical King (From The Boogie Down Bronx)
Fresh Records, 1987
Brotman & Garston, Studio Zed (Design)
Frank Linder (Photo)

16 SEP

Digital Underground
Sons Of The P
Tommy Boy, 1991
Mark Weinberg (Design)
Victor Hall (Photo)

17 SEP

Audio88
Sternzeichen Hass
Normale Musik, 2017
Robert Winter (Design)

18 SEP

Brand Nubian
Everything Is Everything
Elektra, 1994
Alli (Design)
Ari Marcopoulos (Photo)

19 SEP

Da Bush Babees
Remember We
Reprise Records, 1995
Carolyn Quan, Studio Q (Design)
Richard Rose (Photo)

20 SEP

K-Cloud And The Crew And M.C. Valentine
Every Body Dance / Kickin It On The Dock Of The Bay
Cloud 9 Records, 1989
Cover Artists Unknown

21 SEP

The Beat Pimps
Singles
Good Child Records, 2006
Cover Artists Unknown

22 SEP

Buckshot LeFonque
Columbia, 1994
Cover Artists Unknown

23 SEP

Run DMC
Mary Mary
Profile Records, 1988
Run DMC (Design)

24 SEP

* Sep 25th, 1973
John Austin
Watts (California)

Ras Kass
Soul On Ice (Remix) / Marinatin'
Priority Records, 1996
Brian Cross (Photo)

25 SEP

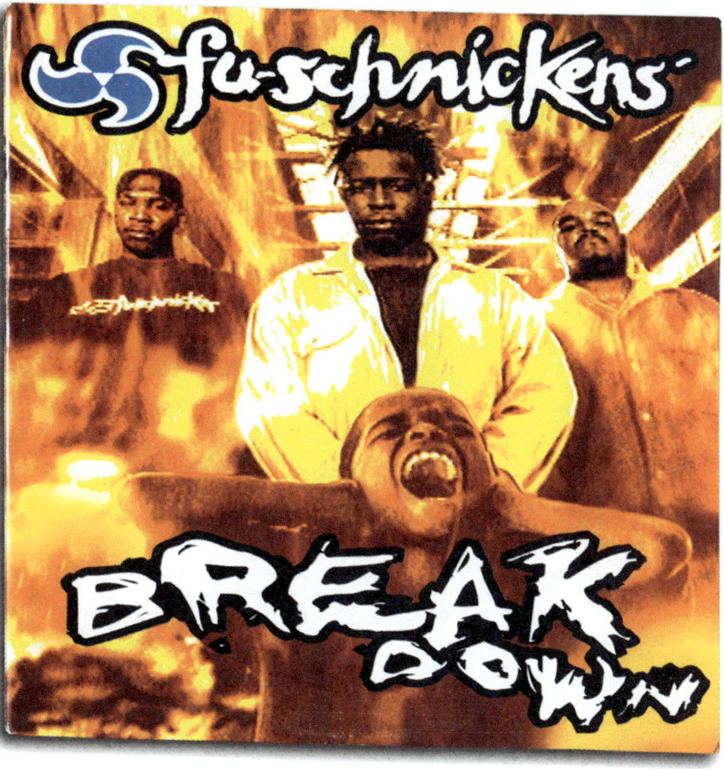

Fu-Schnickens
Breakdown
Jive, 1994
ZombArt:NG (Design)
Marcus Nispel (Photo)

26 SEP

A Tribe Called Quest
People's Instinctive Travels And The Paths Of Rhythm
Jive, 1990
ZombArt DMS (Design)
Bryant Peters (Illustration)

27 SEP

† Sep 28th, 2022
Artis Leon Ivey Jr.
Los Angeles (California)

Coolio
Fantastic Voyage
Tommy Boy, 1994
Erwin Gorostiza (Design)
Michael Miller (Photo)

28 SEP

Elo & MF Saje
5-12 19-1 01
Sichtexot, 2021
Tim Paschedag (Design)

29 SEP

* Sep 30th, 1962
Marlon Williams
Queens (New York City)

Marley Marl
The Symphony
Cold Chillin', 1989
Cover Artists Unknown

Various Artists
Break Dancing
Arcade, 1983
Ruud de Kemp (Design)

01 OCT

* Oct 2nd, 1973
Sascha Reimann
Neuwied (Germany)

Ferris MC
Flash For Ferris MC
Yo Mama's Recording, 2001
Marcnesium (Design)
Mika Väisänen (Photo)

02 OCT

* Oct 3rd, 1975
Talib "Kweli" Greene
Brooklyn (New York City)

Talib Kweli & Hi Tek
Move Somethin'
Rawkus, 2000
Arnold Steiner (Design)
Anderson Ballantyne (Photo)

Nobodys Face
Niemandsland
Four Music, 2016
Bastian Wienecke (Design)
Maxim Rosenbauer (Photo)

04 OCT

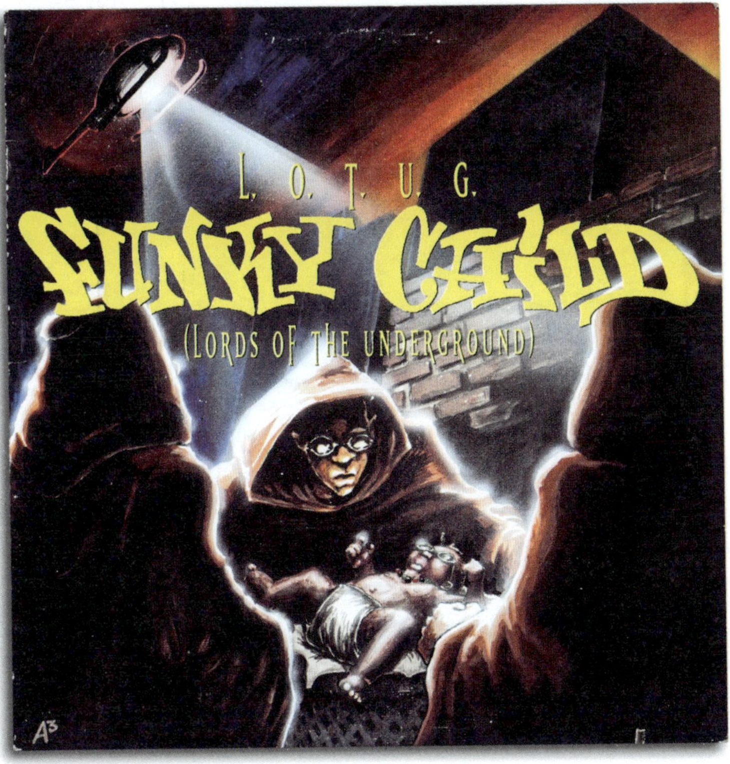

Lords Of The Underground
Funky Child
Pendulum Records, 1992
Ron Jaramillo (Design)

05 OCT

* Oct 6th, 1964
Rahzel Manely
Queens (New York City)

Rahzel
All I Know
MCA Records, 1999
Cover Artists Unknown

06 OCT

Degiheugi
Endless Smile
Endless Smile Records, 2015
Dulk (Design)

07 OCT

Gang Starr
Daily Operation
Cooltempo, 1992
Marc Cozza (Design)
Christopher Edward Martin (Photo)

08 OCT

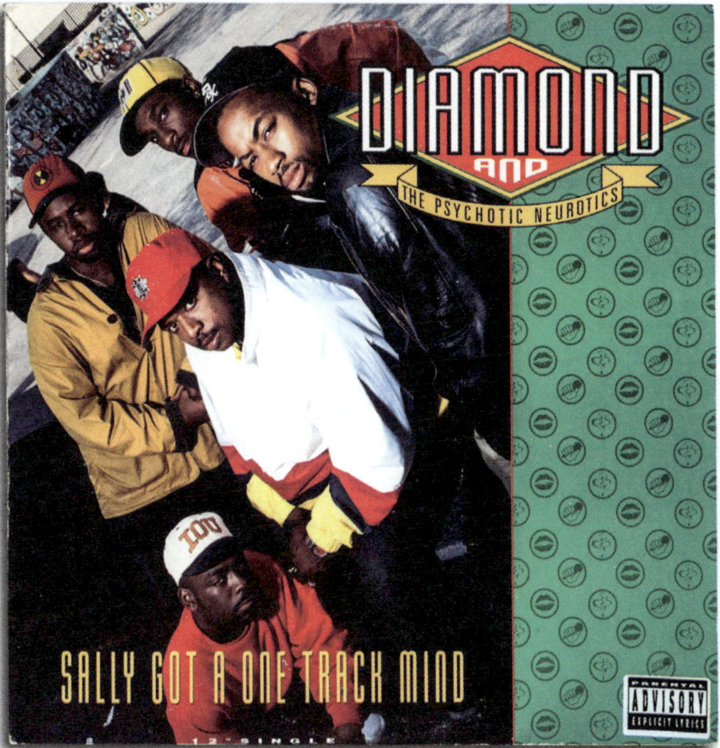

Diamond And The Psychotic Neurotics
Sally Got A One Track Mind
Chemistry Records Ltd , 1993
Dave Brubaker (Design)
Clifton Brett (Photo)

09 OCT

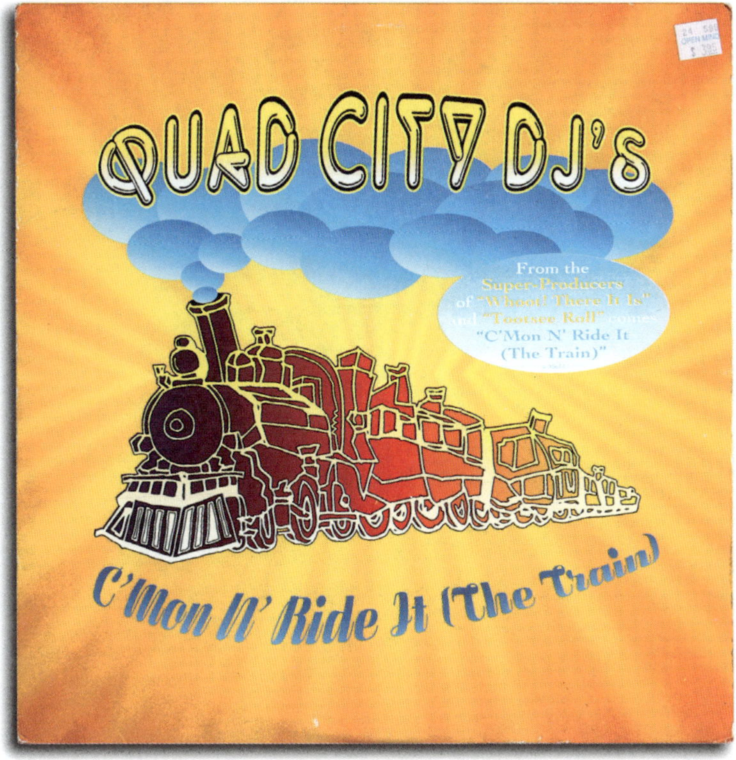

Quad City DJ's
C'mon N' Ride It (The Train)
Atlantic, 1996
Cover Artists Unknown

10 OCT

* Oct 11th, 1971
Lana Michele Moorer
Queens (New York City)

MC Lyte
Eyes On This
First Priority Music, 1989
Bob Defrin (Design)
Robert Manella (Photo)

11 OCT

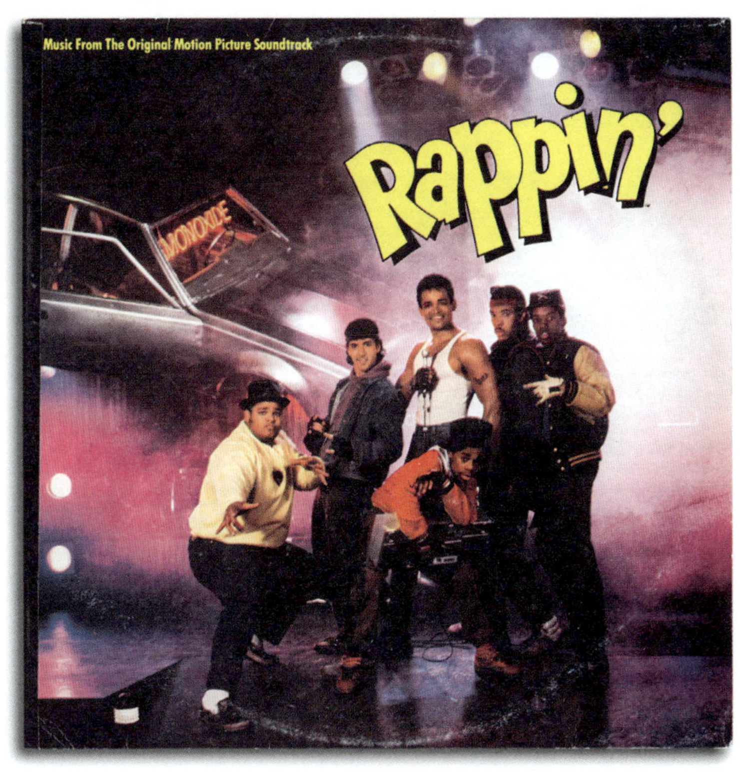

Original Soundtrack
Rappin'
Atlantic, 1985
Tzachi Ostrovsky (Photo)

12 OCT

Supreme Ntm
1993, J'Appuie Sur La Gachette...
Epic, 2014
Artcore Design (Design)

13 OCT

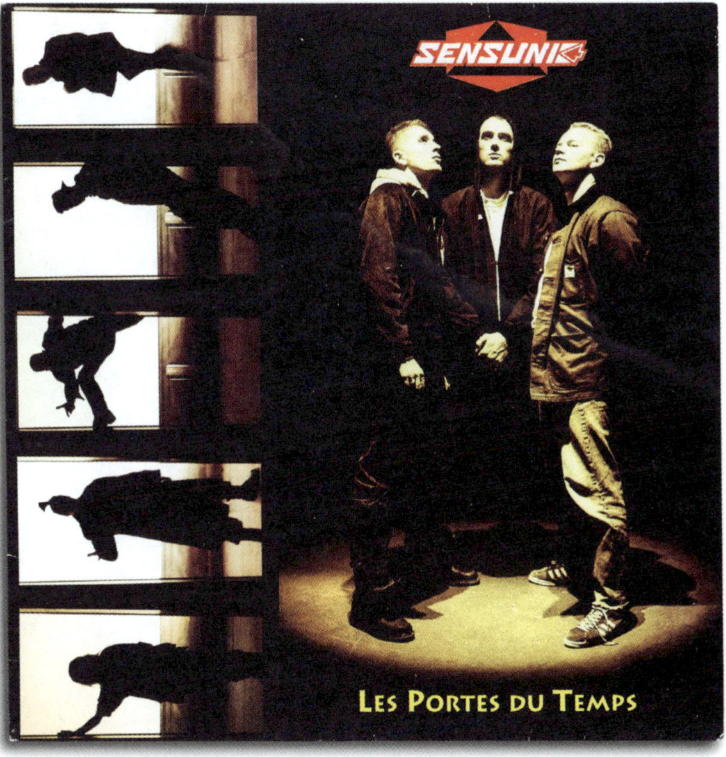

Sens Unik
Les Portes Du Temps
Unik Records, 1992
G. Antonioni, Pierre Fantis, S. Kutty (Photo)

14 OCT

Gang Starr
Jazz Thing
CBS, 1990
Cover Artists Unknown

15 OCT

7evenThirty
The Problem
Mello Music Group, 2014
Cover Artists Unknown

16 OCT

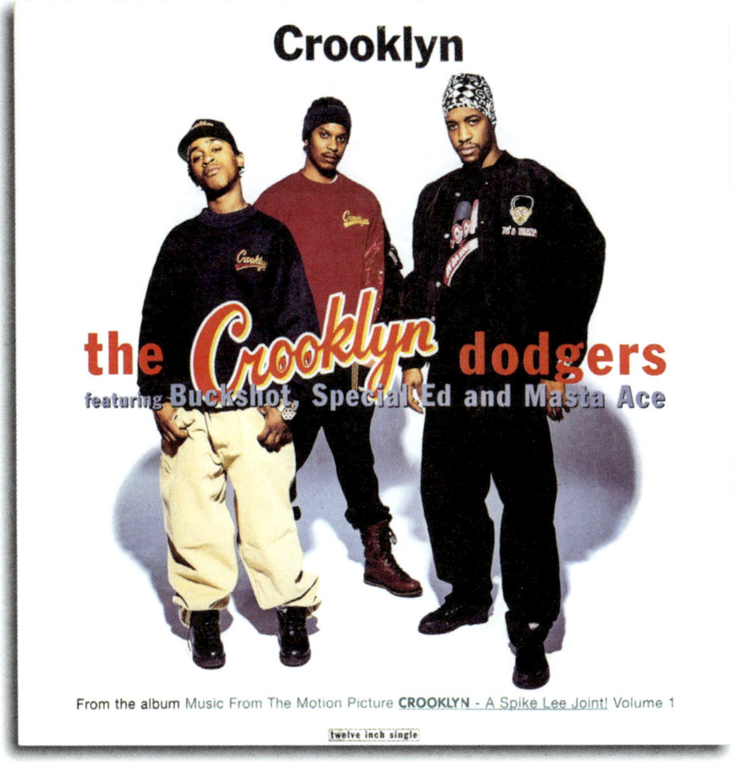

The Crooklyn Dodgers
Crooklyn
MCA Records, 1994
Cover Artists Unknown

17 OCT

LSD
Watch Out For The Third Rail
Rhythm Attack Productions, 1991
Cover Artists Unknown

18 OCT

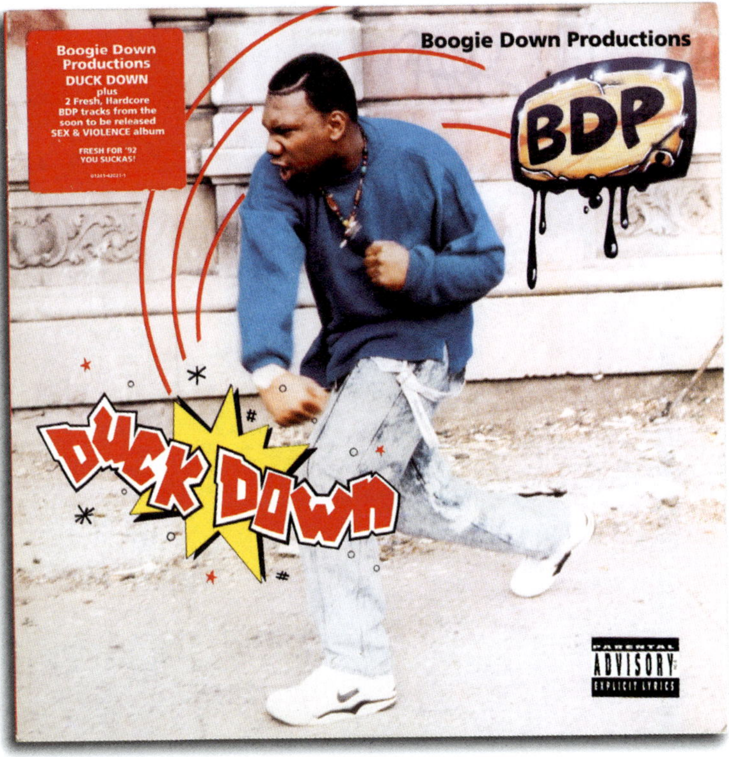

Boogie Down Productions
Duck Down
Jive, 1992
ZombaArt JK (Design)
Gary Spector (Photo)

19 OCT

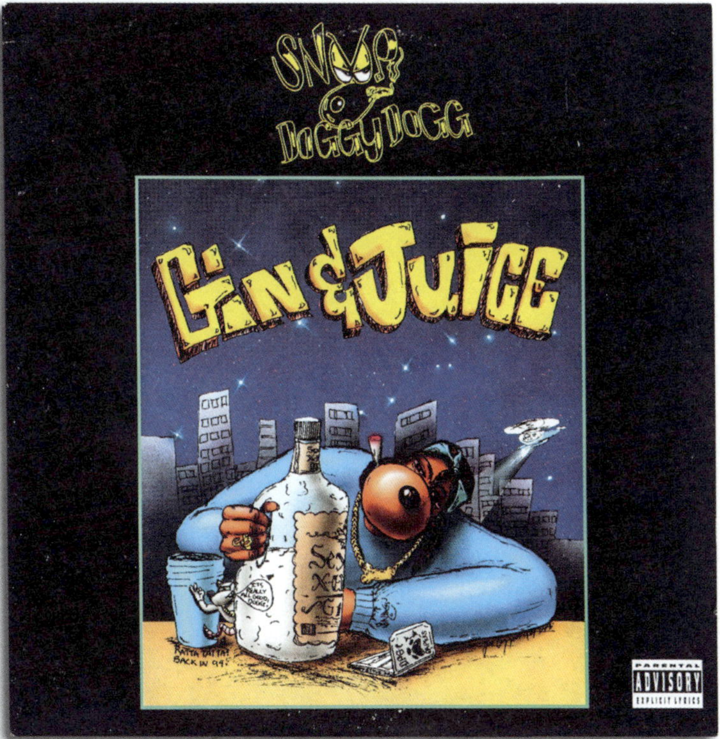

* Oct 20th, 1971
Calvin Cordozar Broadus Jr.
Long Beach (California)

Snoop Doggy Dogg
Gin And Juice
Death Row Records, 1994
Cover Artists Unknown

20 OCT

Roots Manuva
Dub Come Save Me
Big Data Recordings, 2002
Foxy (Photo)

21 OCT

Digital Underground
Doowutchyalike
BCM Records, 1989
Rackadelic-Gregory Jacobs (Illustration)

22 OCT

Skatemaster Tate And The Concrete Crew
Do The Skate
4th & Broadway, 1991
Cover Artists Unknown

23 OCT

Sonne Ra & Eloquent
Im in Hier
Sichtexot, 2021
Fley Gramb (Photo)

Herr Von Grau
Freiflug
Grautöne Records, 2013
Cover Artists Unknown

25 OCT

Ozomatli
Saturday Night / Ya Viene El Sol (The Beatle Bob Remix)
Cover Artists Unknown

26 OCT

BLINDED
BY
THE
NEON

FERGE X
FISHERMAN

Ferge X Fisherman
Blinded By The Neon
Initiative Musik GmbH, 2020
Cover Artists Unknown

27 OCT

Dennis Real
Pelican Valley
12 Drunkies, 2021
Cover Artists Unknown

28 OCT

Blood Of Abraham
Future Profits
Ruthless Records, 1993
Cover Artists Unknown

29 OCT

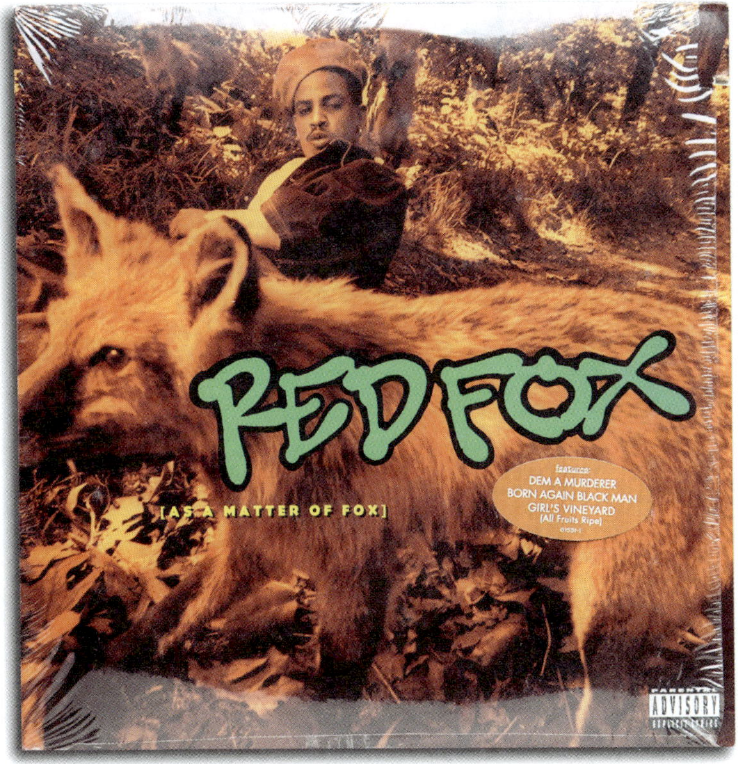

Red Fox
As A Matter Of Fox
Elektra, 1993
Alli (Design)
Michael Lavine (Photo)

30 OCT

Krawanesia
Campur
Not On Label, 2017
Pascal Maurer (Illustration)

31 OCT

THE ART OF Soul COVERS
WORLD'S FIRST VINYL CALENDAR
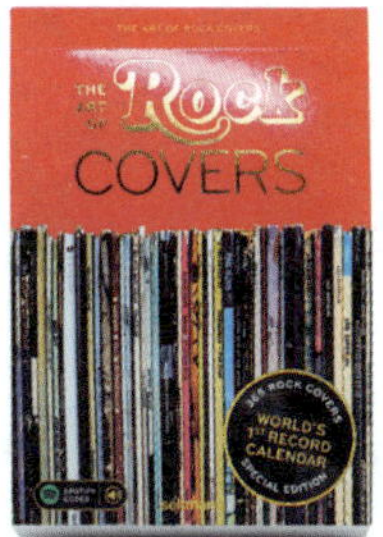
THE ART OF Rock COVERS
WORLD'S 1ST RECORD CALENDAR

THE ART OF JAZZ COVERS
WORLD'S 1ST RECORD CALENDAR
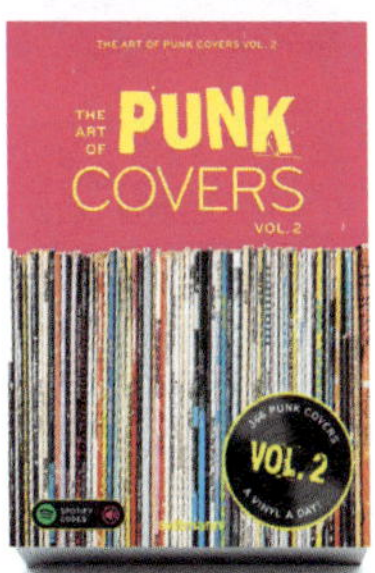
THE ART OF PUNK COVERS
VOL. 2
VOL. 2

THE ART OF SOUNDTRACK COVERS
CALENDAR
WORLD'S 1ST RECORD CALENDAR

THE ART OF REGGAE COVERS
WORLD'S FIRST VINYL CALENDAR

THE ART OF METAL COVERS
VOL. 2
WORLD'S FIRST VINYL CALENDAR

THE ART OF HIP-HOP COVERS
WORLD'S 1ST RECORD CALENDAR

THE ART OF HIP-HOP COVERS
VOL. 2
WORLD'S FIRST VINYL CALENDAR

Thes One
Noonen
Tres Records, 2004
Cover Artists Unknown

01 NOV

Blackalicious
Make You Feel That Way / Sky Is Falling
MCA Records, 2002
Cover Artists Unknown

02 NOV

Oddisee
The Beauty In All
Mello Music Group, 2013
Cover Artists Unknown

03 NOV

Freshco & Miz
We Don't Play
Tommy Boy, 1990
Kristine Larsen (Photo)

04 NOV

The Brand New Heavies
Heavy Rhyme Experience: Vol. 1
Delicious Vinyl, 1992
Salomon Emquies (Photo)

05 NOV

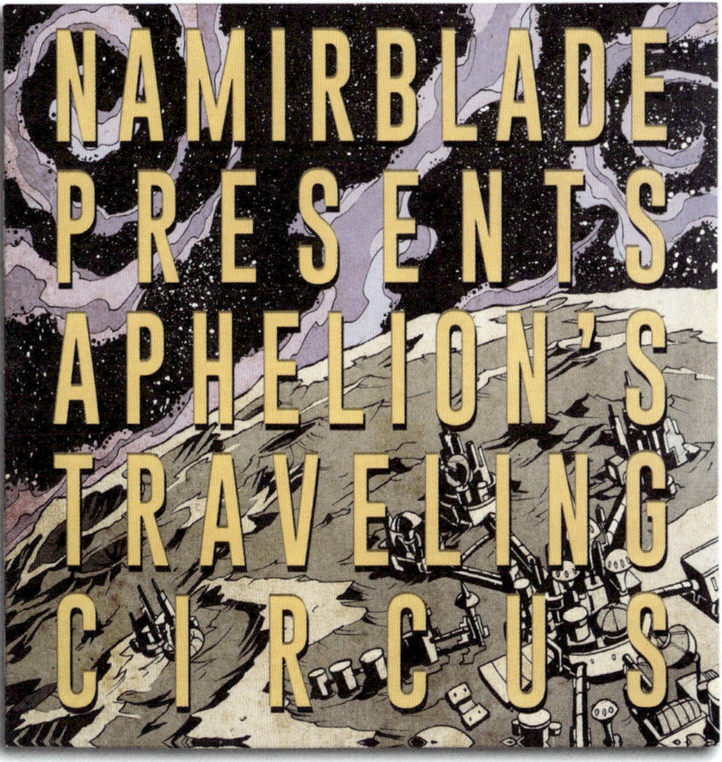

NAMIRBLADE
PRESENTS
APHELION'S
TRAVELING
CIRCUS

Namir Blade
Aphelion's Traveling Circus
Mello Music Group, 2020
Cover Artists Unknown

06 NOV

Pmd
Rugged-N-Raw
Relativity, 1996
Julian Alexander (Design)
Daniel "Castro" Hastings (Photo)

07 NOV

Hardnoise
Serve Tea, Then Murder
Music Of Life, 1991
Duo-creatics (Design)

08 NOV

* Nov 9th, 1969
Lolita Shante Gooden
Queens (New York City)

The Real Roxanne
Roxanne's On A Roll
Urban, 1989
Amy Bennick (Design)
Peter Bodtke (Photo)

09 NOV

DJ Spinna
Heavy Beats Volume 1
Rawkus, 1999
Nobody, Phase 2 (Design)
Franck Khalfoun (Photo)

10 NOV

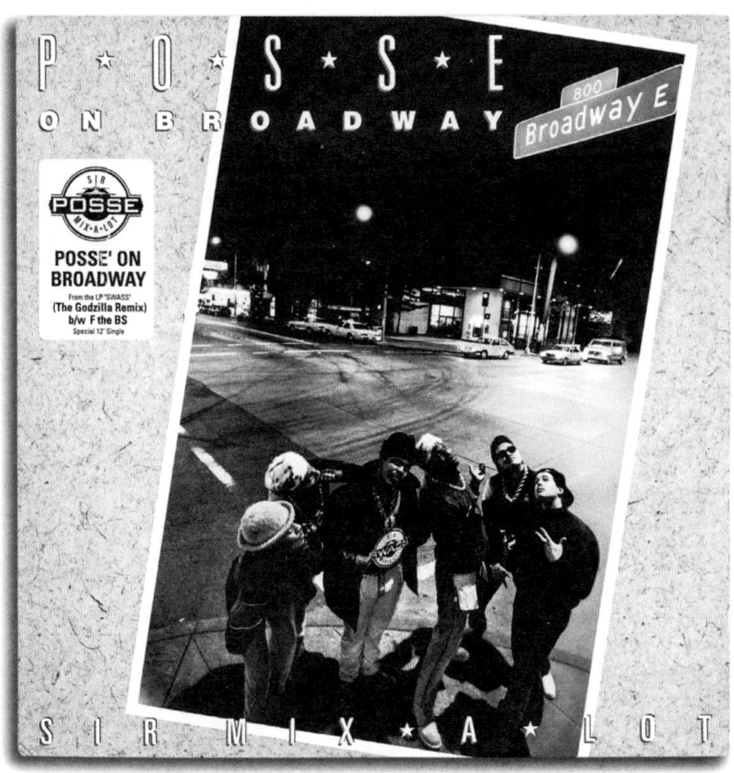

Sir Mix-A-Lot
Posse' On Broadway
Nastymix Records, 1988
Terada Design (Design)
Wall Street Productions (Photo)

11 NOV

Onyx
Black Rock
X Ray Records, 2018
Feo (Design)

12 NOV

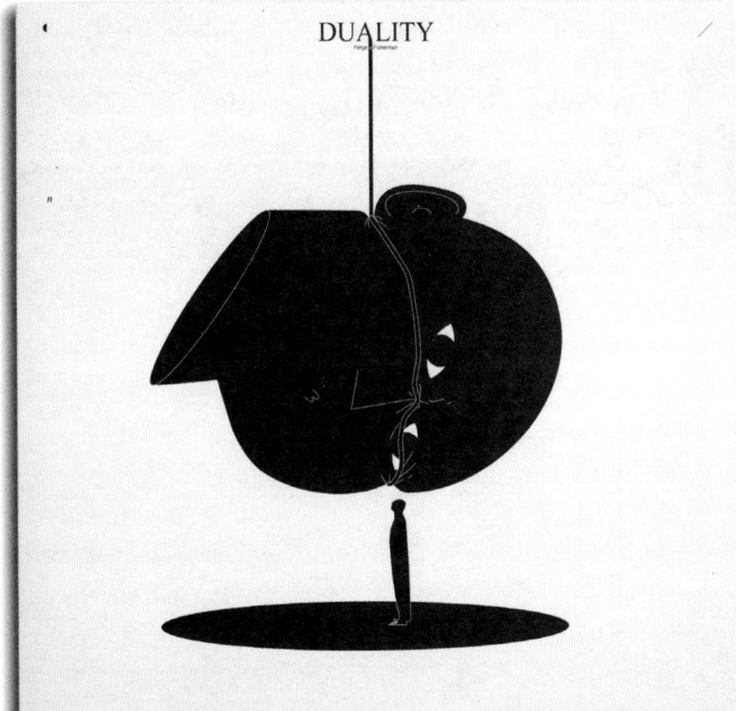

Ferge X Fisherman
Duality
Ferge X Fisherman GbR, 2022
Cover Artists Unknown

13 NOV

Rasco
Take It Back Home / Major League (Remix)
Stones Throw Records, 1998
MC.III (Design)

14 NOV

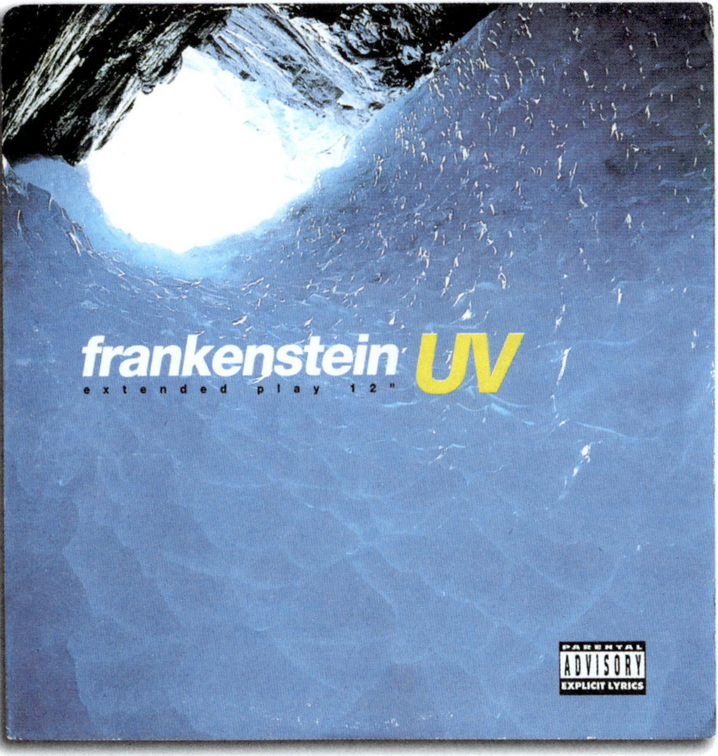

Frankenstein
UV
Knowledge of Soul, 1997
Mental Oriental (Design)

15 NOV

Haiyti
Montenegro Zero
Universal Music Group, 2018
Cover Artists Unknown

16 NOV

Stf
Keine Effekte / Knock It Off!
Blitz Vinyl, 1994
MZEE Graphics, Kotthoff (Design)

17 NOV

Hen-Gee & Evil-E
Brothers
Pendulum Records, 1991
Janet Perr (Design)
Michael Lavine (Photo)

18 NOV

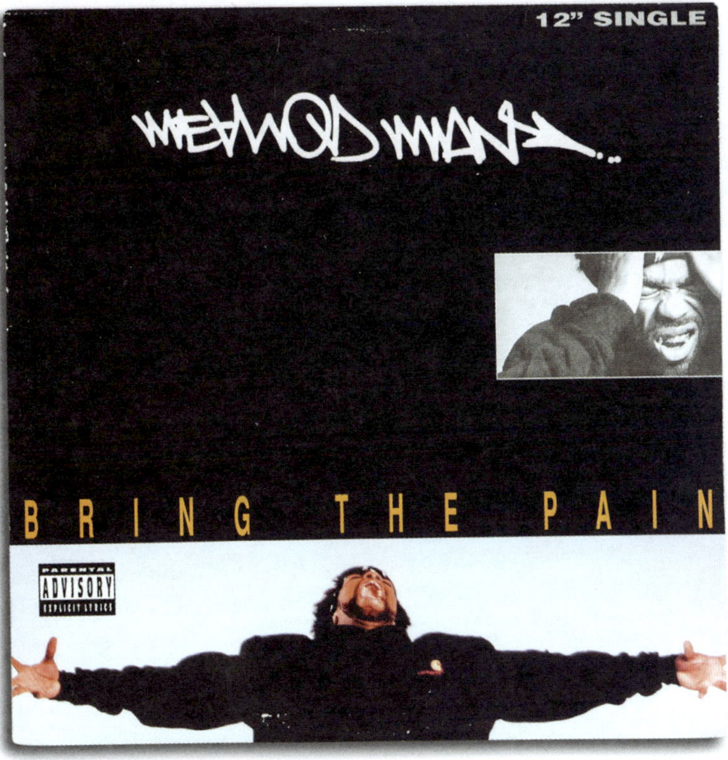

Method Man
Bring The Pain
Def Jam Recordings, 1994
Cover Artists Unknown

19 NOV

Retrogott & Hulkhodn
Kontemporärkontamination
Entbs, 2018
Cover Artists Unknown

20 NOV

The Pharcyde
Labcabincalifornia
Delicious Vinyl, 1995
Truly Rain (Design)
Block (Photo)

21 NOV

Blacksheep
Flavor The Month
Mercury, 1991
Dana Brandwein (Design)

22 NOV

Ice-T
Colors
Warner Bros. Records, 1988
Glen E. Friedman (Photo)

23 NOV

Souls Of Mischief
93 'Til Infinity
Jive, 1993
ZombaArt NG (Design)
Michael Miller (Photo)

24 NOV

Plattenpapzt Feat: Tefla & Jaleel
Wenn Zonis Reisen...
Jive, 2000
NUI.graffngraphBetonplaza 4000/30 / Düsseldorf (Design)
Photo Schiko (Photo)

25 NOV

Sido
Mein Block
Aggro Berlin, 2004
Specter-Aggressives Aussehen (Design)
NBK-Aggressives Aussehen (Illustration)

26 NOV

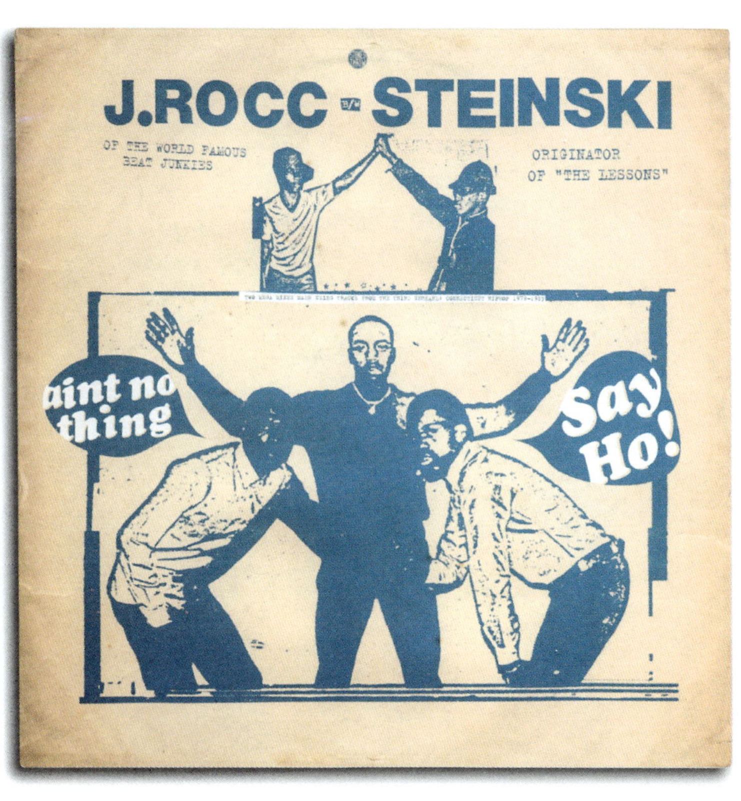

J.Rocc/Steinski
Ain't No Thing / Say Ho!
Stones Throw Records, 2004
Super-J (Design)

27 NOV

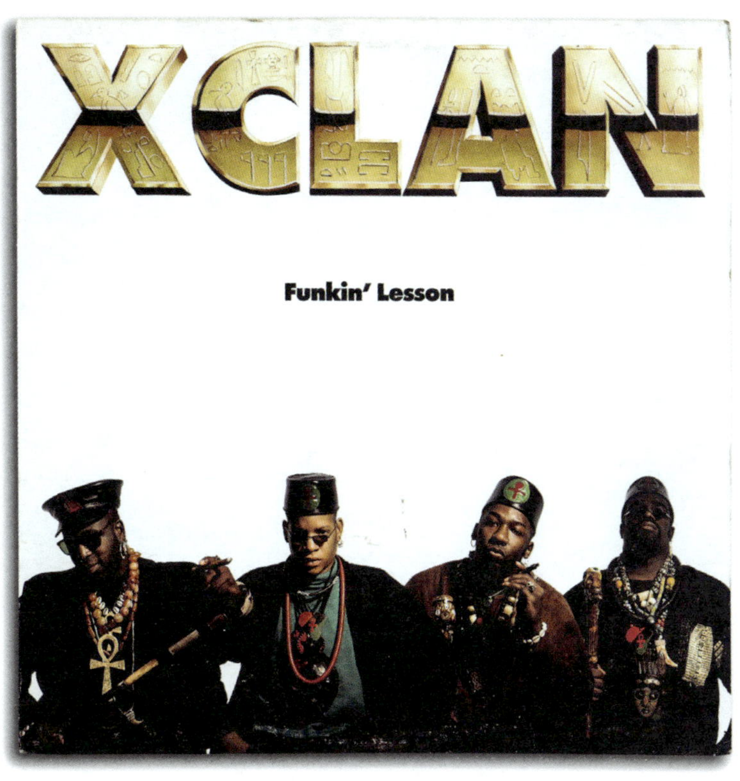

X-Clan
Funkin' Lesson
4th & Broadway, 1990
Cover Artists Unknown

KC Flight
Planet E
RCA, 1989
Preston Phillip (Photo)

Retrogott & Sonne Ra
Sonnengott
Entbs, 2018
Chlodwigplatz Pütz Money (Photo)

30 NOV

Marteria
Roswell
Four Music, 2017
Specter Berlin (Design)
Zentrale (Illustration)

01 DEC

Guru
Illkid Records
Payday, 1995
Gary Saint Clare (Design)

02 DEC

Sandy B

AMAJOVI JOVI

ICE 013

SIDE A

AMAJOVI JOVI
STUDENT NIGHT
DEDICATION

SIDE B

LIFAKE (DOGGY STYLE) *
PARTY TIME **
AMAJOVI JOVI (INSTRUMENTAL)

Sandy B
Amajovi Jovi
Invisible City Editions, 2017
Zeitype (Design)

03 DEC

* Dec 4th, 1969
Shawn Corey Carter as-Jay Z
New York City

Jaz
Hawaiian Sophie
EMI USA, 1989
Timothy White (Photo)

04 DEC

KUSO GVKI
Kuso Gaki Type Beats
Not On label, 2021
Cover Artists Unknown

05 DEC

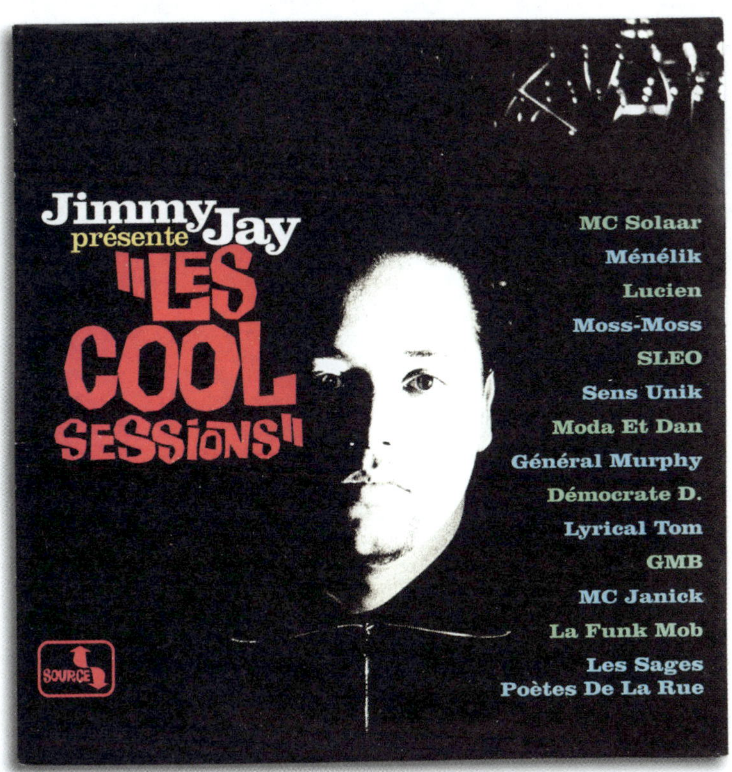

Jimmy Jay
"Les Cool Sessions"
Source, 1993
Swifty Typografix (Design)
Philippe Bordas (Photo)

06 DEC

Various Artists
Funky Break Essentials
FunkWar Records, 1998
Gismo (Design)

07 DEC

Donald D
Let The Horns Blow
Sire, 1991
Dirk Walter (Design)
Mario Castellanos (Photo)

Andy Cooper
Room To Breathe
Unique, 2016
Chrispop (Design)
Tina Hakim (Photo)

Pete Rock
Petestrumentals
BBE, 2001
Thomas ‚Bad Shoes' Mc Callion (Design)
Dave Jewell, Vincent McDonald (Photo)

10 DEC

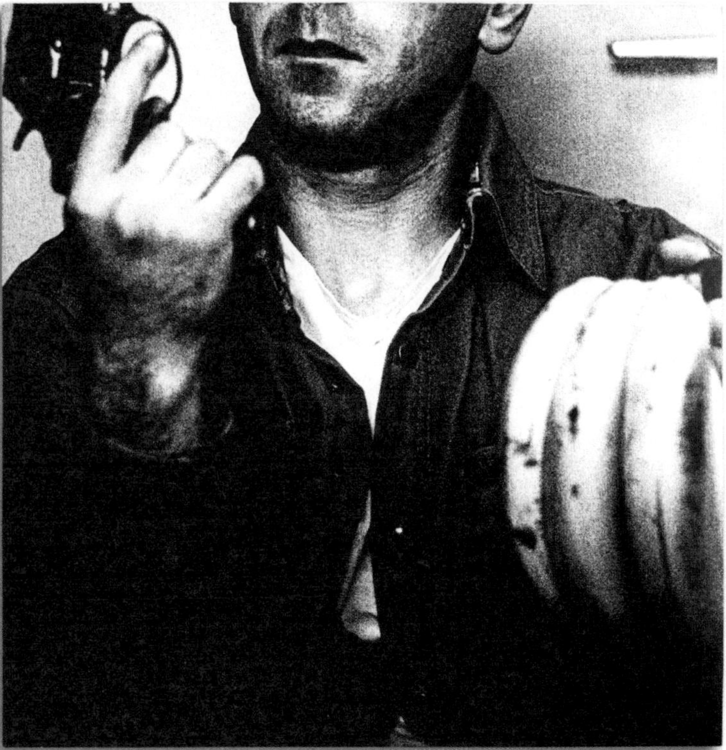

Elo & Torky
Modus Minus
Sichtexot, 2020
Jeremias Diekmann (Design)
Anton Pfurtscheller (Photo)

11 DEC

* Dec 12th, 1968
M.C. La Kim
Newark (New Jersey)

Lakim Shabazz
Pure Righteousness
Tuff City, 1988
Ramona Mariano (Design)
Ebet Roberts (Photo)

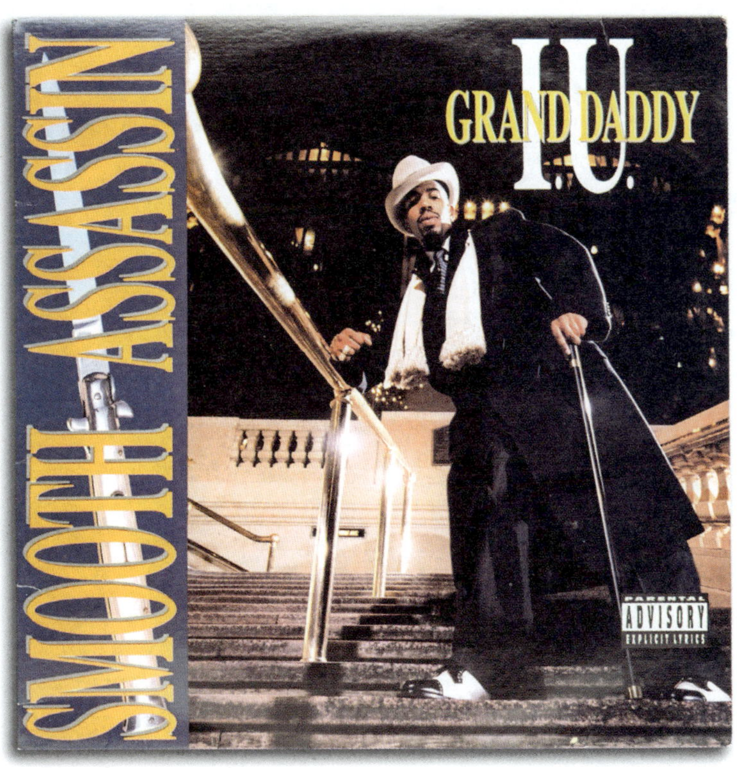

† Dec 13th, 2022
Ayub Bey
New York City

Grand Daddy I.U.
Smooth Assassin
Cold Chillin', 1990
George Du Bose (Design)

13 DEC

* Dec 14th, 1968
Roger McBride
Los Angeles (California)

King Tee
Bass / Ko Rock Stuff
Capitol Records, 1988
Glen E. Friedman (Photo)

Digable Planets
Blowout Comb
Pendulum Records, 1994
Henry Marquez (Design)
Daniela Federici (Illustration)

15 DEC

Doctor J.R. Kool & The Other Roxannes
The Complete Story Of Roxanne...The Album
Compleat Records, 1985
Gerry Giles (Photo)

16 DEC

Fort Greene Chronicles

51 Copyright © 1998 Fort Greene Chronicles NEW YORK, WEDNESDAY beyond the greater New York metropolitan area.

EXTRA, EXTRA!!

The Album In Stores
Summer, 1998

PAULA PERRY

Paula Perry
Extra, Extra!!
Motown, 1998
Cover Artists Unknown

17 DEC

DJ Honda Feat. Mos Def
Travellin' Man
Relativity, 1998
Cover Artists Unknown

18 DEC

* Dec 19th, 1977
Damy Sorge
Hamburg (Germany)

Samy Deluxe
Berühmte letzte Worte
Vertigo, 2016
Benjamin Kakrow, Typeholics (Illustration)

19 DEC

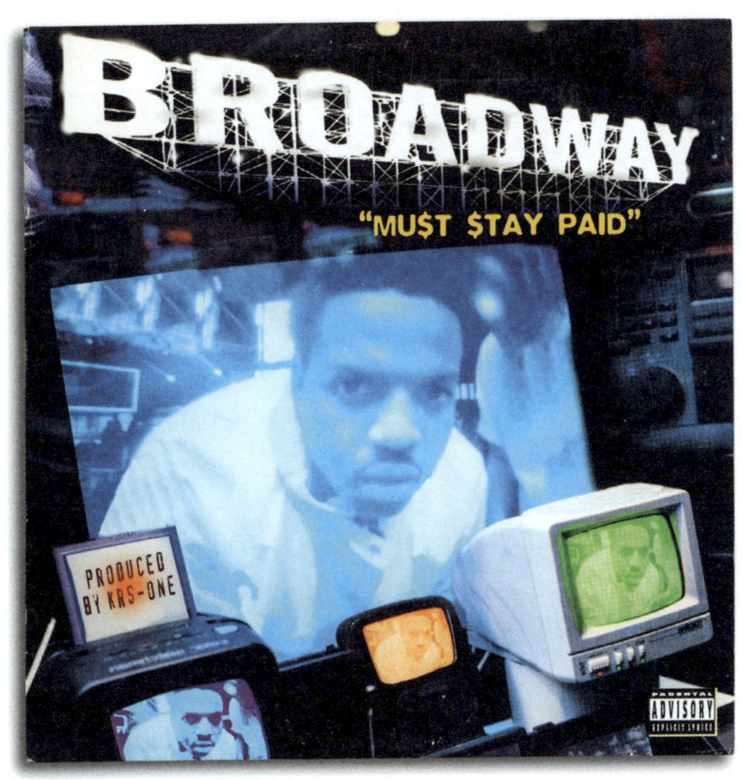

Broadway
Mu$t $tay Paid
Wreck Records, 1996
Merge One (Design)
Michael Benabib (Photo)

20 DEC

Ruthless Bastards
Murder We Wrote / Ruthless Bastards
Flowmaster Recordings, 1997
Cover Artists Unknown

21 DEC

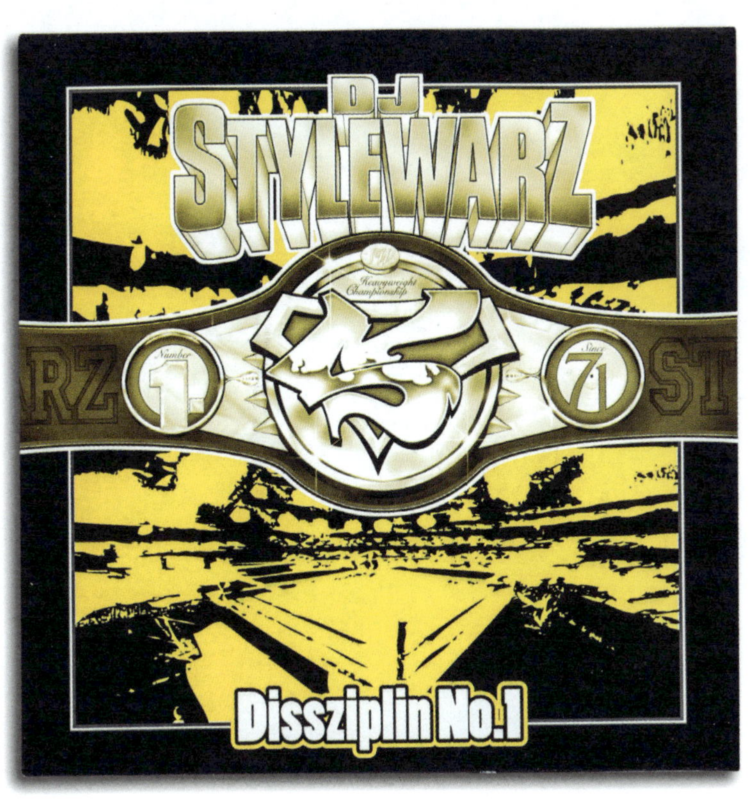

DJ Stylewarz
Dissziplin No. 1
Eimsbush, 2000
Dee One (Design)
Typeholics (Illustration)

22 DEC

Lifers Group
Hollywood Basic, 1991
Cover Artists Unknown

23 DEC

Run DMC
Christmas In Hollis
Get on Down, 2014
Alfredo Rico-Dimas (Design)
Keith Haring (Illustration)

24 DEC

De La Soul
Millie Pulled A Pistol On Santa / Keepin' The Faith
Tommy Boy, 1991
Erwin Gorostiza (Design)
Richard Hernández (Illustration)

25 DEC

Too Strong
Rabenschwarze Nacht
Tribehouse Recordings, 1993
Tribehaus-Graphics (Design)
Zonic (Illustration)

26 DEC

Marius No. 1
The Record Player EP
Chiefrocker Records, 2004
Martin Hennig (Design)
Mika Väisänen (Photo)

27 DEC

Paulina Urban & Krawanesia
Saudara
Membran, 2019n)
Pascal Maurer (Illustration)

28 DEC

Classic der Dicke & Soulmade **Body Mass Index**

Classic Der Dicke & Soulmade
Body Mass Index
Daily Concept, 2017
Chezz.One (Design)
Martin Barrientos (Illustration)

29 DEC

Al Dobson Jr.
Sounds From The Village Vol.2
IZWID Records, 2019
Brandy Flower (Design)
Justin McNulty (Illustration)

30 DEC

Galv
Of The 3 Moonz
Muther Manufaktur, 2016
Jacob Eisinger, Rob Hak (Design)

31 DEC

Imprint

THE ART OF HIP HOP COVERS VOL. 2

Seltmann Publishers
Berlin, Germany
www.seltmannpublishers.com
info@seltmannpublishers.com

Cover Selection & Background Research:
Bernd Jonkmanns

Thanks to Johnny Jonkmanns, Mitra Kassai, Dieter Braun, Götz Bühler, Simon Kupfer and a special thanks for the great selection from DJ Mad (Beginner) out of his amazing record collection.

Art Direction: Sandro Heindel, Stefan Küstner

We thank everyone involved for their unique artistic work that made this project possible. If you have any questions or suggestions, please do not hesitate to contact us personally.

This project is an homage to the great and glorious decade of vinyl records and their wonderfully designed covers. With this project, we aim to showcase and preserve the covers as well as their high level of artistic power and profound meaningfulness. Every cover has been selected from personal vinyl collections and individually photographed.

Please note:
Not all bands present themselves on Spotify, so there are various albums without a code.

ISBN 978-3-949070-60-0